HOW TO SURVIVE YOUR FINANCIAL CRISIS™

A Compilation of Critical Information from Experts on:
Bankruptcy ~ Reverse Mortgage ~ Mortgage Modification
Strategies for the Unemployed & Small Business Owner
~ Divorce ~ Free Help for Special Needs Children
& Seniors ~ ID Theft~ IRS Issues... *AND LOTS MORE*

AF738112

Are you unemployed?
Are you the struggling business owner?
Are you overwhelmed with debt and monthly bills?
Are you stressed by the financial effects of divorce?
Are you looking to understand:
mortgage modification; bankruptcy or how to handle plummeting home values?

COMPILED & EDITED BY VIVIAN GASPAR

IF SO... OPEN HERE

The content within this book is not intended to take the place of a consultation with a qualified professional regarding the readers' specific circumstances.

The book's ISBN catagories are:
Finance, Personal, Self-Help Technique

ISBN 978-0-9832121-0-2

Published by B&L Printing Co. Inc.
Hillsborough, NJ

For information, address:
Carpe 28, LLC
275 Route 10 East, Suite 220
Succasunna, NJ 07876

Printed in the United States of America

Look for this symbol for Vivian's Picks for notable tid-bits!

Forward

As someone who has worked individually, in the last two years, with over two hundred families in financial crisis as the Public Relations Director and Mortgage Modification Specialist with the legal office of V. James Castiglia in New Jersey, I found myself hearing similar stories and repeatedly giving the same advice. In addition to assisting couples in proper completion of mortgage modification applications, I also dispensed advice on a range of topics where I had developed expertise, since my experiences include having owned a marketing company and being a recruiter. I also help people decipher their current mortgages since I was a mortgage loan officer for many years.

Part of my responsibilities as Mr. Castiglia's Public Relations Director was to give speeches to civic organizations such as the Lions Clubs and Rotary Clubs at their locations in New Jersey. After many of these speeches, where I would educate the members of these clubs, I had been approached to spread my information to a wider audience and to consider writing a book.

In February of 2010, I started to give the idea of writing a book on mortgage modification and the foreclosure process more serious consideration. However, I wanted to have a wider impact. As I gave this idea more thought, I concluded that I could help a wider base of people in crisis if I covered a broad subject base. As I started an outline of chapters and topics I wanted to see included in my book I immediately thought of all the business contacts I had accumulated over the years. This book is my opportunity to bring to you the knowledge of seasoned professionals on specific topics where they have a great deal of expertise. It includes contributions from 27 professionals who have written 38 chapters.

My first book, "How to Survive Your Financial Crisis", was released February 2011 with the Spanish translation set to release in the Summer of 2012. A second book on financial topics as well as that book's Spanish version to be released Fall of 2012. I also envision the translation of both books into the top 10 most popular languages with international sales and marketing through the website:
www.howtosurviveyourfinancialcrisis.com.

For many years now I have educated people on topics ranging from "Mortgage Trivia for Everyone" to "Identity Theft and Understanding the Basics of Credit Scores" to "Understanding Mortgage Modification and the Foreclosure Process". Now I want to bring to people the most concisely worded information on a variety of the most critical financial survival topics which everyone can use at one low price.

Please enjoy the journey of learning contained within the following pages and please e-mail me at Vivian@howtosurviveyourfinancialcrisis.com telling me how the information in this book has helped to improve your life.

Thank you and happy reading!

Vivian Gaspar

Dedication

This book, and all my dreams of helping as many people as possible, though education on a broad variety of topics is due to my love for the people closest to me. My mother had always dreamed I would become a writer by profession, (specifically a journalist) since I had started writing short stories and poems when I was very young. (I was accepted into the Accelerated Creative Writing Program at Montclair State University when I was 15.) I actually had always attributed my entrepreneurial spirit to my father. I always had been inspired by my father as I had seen him try his hand at many businesses ever since I was young and throughout my adulthood. Therefore, I am quite happy to say that this book, to be the first in a series, can be attributed to both my parents who I love deeply.

I would also like to dedicate this book to my husband, Richard, who has always been very supportive of my entrepreneurial endeavors.

Also, I am also very appreciative and grateful to have worked with V. James Castiglia in the mortgage modification arena. I appreciate Jim Castiglia's hard work and dedication to not just his clients, but I also really enjoyed learning from him in the countless client meetings I had the privilege to have been witness to. Mr. Castiglia's broad knowledge base and how he delivers that knowledge in a comforting and tireless fashion is always an inspiration to me. I felt driven in my work because of it. Without Mr. Castiglia and my experiences working for and with him and his exceptional staff, this book would never have been possible. Thank you, Jim!

Vivian Gaspar

Acknowledgements

As the developer of this very inclusive reference book I would really like to take the time to express my gratitude to the over 30 people without whom this book could never have come to fruition.

First and foremost, I really want to acknowledge and thank my parents. My husband of the last 10 years and companion of the last 22 years who has been instrumental in my being able to bring this book to its completion because it really has been an on-going challenge to support my time and energy which needed to be devoted to this project while I have been working full time for the attorney as the Mortgage Modification Specialist and Public Relations Director.

Naturally, I am extremely grateful to the 27 authors who were very generous with their time and sharing their expertise. I believe that these gracious individuals should be commended for their generosity, since all of them have very busy professional practices.

I would also like to thank the other talented individuals who I have had the good fortune to have on my team: Regina Barletta, the Director of Desktop Publishing at B&L Printing who has been very instrumental throughout this entire process as well as Gerry Harris my publisher and owner of B&L Printing. I would also like to thank my very talented editor — Elaine Bloom. Another critical member of my team is Jim Castiglia, who is my staff attorney and contributing co-author on several chapters and the reason for this book's very existence. Thank you very much also to Veronica Yankowski, my staff photographer. Also, I really appreciate the tireless efforts of Allison Freeman who is my Public Relations Director.

I also really appreciated all of the hard work of my website devoloper Camille Re who created the website for this book, www.howtosurviveyourfinancialcrisis.com.

Vivian Gaspar

Table of Contents

Section 1

Personal Crisis -
Protect Your Identity & Eliminate Personal Debt:

ID Theft ~ by Vivian Gaspar .... p. 13

THE BASICS: How & Why to Have Good Credit
~ by Vivian Gaspar .... p. 19

Debt Settlement ~ by Rocco Sileo .... p. 25

Section 2

Practical Help For The Unemployed:

Lost Your Job? Understand Your
COBRA Benefits ~ by Harry Herbst .... p. 35

How to Get Your Recruiter to Focus
On You ~ by Joanne Lucas .... p. 41

How To Ace Your Next Job Interview
~ by Joanne Lucas .... p. 47

Can't Find a Job? Direct Marketing -
A Real Income Alternative ~ by Camille Re .... p. 55

How Anyone Can Make Money
From Home ~ by Vivian Gaspar .... p. 65

Section 3

Valuable Information For All Business Owners & Sales Professionals:

~Special Introduction by Ted Fattoross: "You Are Not Your Business Card"~

How To Get Your Business to Survive Tough Economies ~ by Neil Pinkman .... p. 79

Your Business Plan - Yes, It Can Be A Daily Tool ~ by Jack Bleiberg, CPA .... p. 85

In Person Business Networking ~ by Philip Doyle .... p. 93

Health and Life Insurance for the Business Owner ~ by Harry Herbst .... p. 97

Cold Calling Tips for Business Owners and Salespeople ~ by Deborah Anderson .... p. 103

Low/No Cost Benefits to Retain Employees ~ by Katherine Woodfield Hermes...... p. 109

Your Local Printer is Better Than Vista Print? Yes! ~ by Gerry Harris.......................p. 119

Insurances Every Business Owner Must Have ~ by Terrance Coughlin .... p. 123

Practical Marketing For Every Business's Budget ~ by Ronald Hatcher............... p. 129

Mediation for Business Owners ~ by Robert J. McDonnell, MS APM .... p. 143

Merchant Services - Understand Costs & Use to Get New Clients ~ by Frank Gallipoli... p. 151

Alternative Business Financing – Bridge Your Financial Gap ~ by Frank Gallipoli... p. 155

Public Speaking Skills for Business Owners/Sales Professionals ~ by Marlene Waldock .... p. 161

Cash Flow Tips for Your Business ~ by Vito Mazza... p. 167

W2 or 1099 – The Wrong Choice Can Cost You Your Business ~ by James Hyland .... p. 175

<u>Section 4</u>

<u>Critical Information for Those Facing Divorce:</u>

What to Do When He/She Says "I'm Outta Here" ~ by Carolyn Daly, ESQ... p. 183

Divorce Mediation - A Practical Way to Lessen the Cost & Stress ~ by Robert J. McDonnell, MS APM ..... p. 193

<u>Section 5</u>

<u>For Home Owners & Renters Alike Preparing For and Surviving Natural Disasters & Financial Crisis:</u>

Financially Surviving Natural Disasters ~ by Terrance Coughlin .... p. 203

Mortgage Modification – Use It and Save Your Home & Your Sanity ~ by Vivian Gaspar & V. James Castiglia, ESQ. .... p. 209

Understanding The Foreclosure Process – Why To Short Sale vs. Foreclosure ~ by Vivian Gaspar & V. James Castiglia, ESQ. ... p. 215

Reverse Mortgages – A Financial Option for Seniors ~ by Peter Nagy ... p. 223

<u>Section 6</u>

<u>General Finance for Everyone:</u>

About My Mortgage ~ by Stephanie Banks .... p. 231

Bankruptcy – Understand the Basics ~ by Santo Bonanno, ESQ.................... p. 253

Save On Your Energy Bills ~ by Michael Menihan ... p. 259

How a Private Investigator Can Help You Get Money ~ by Alexander Toia, PI...................... p. 265

Free At Home Assistance For Veterans & Their Spouses ~ by Bonnie Laiderman .... p. 273

Government Benefits for Low Income Individuals ~ by Dr. Darsi Beauchamp .... p. 277

Get Special Education Help for Students with Disabilities at No Cost ~ by Dr. Darsi Beauchamp .... p. 283

How to Get an Amazing Education for Low to No Cost ~ by Dr. Darsi Beauchamp ....p. 311

I Owe the IRS… HELP ~ by Jack Bleiberg, CPA..... p. 315

Frequently Asked Tax Questions ~ by Jack Bleiberg, CPA... p. 319

SECTION 1

Personal Crisis - Protect Your Identity & Eliminate Personal Debt

Identity Theft

by Vivian Gaspar

" This is not a question of six degrees of separation – everybody knows somebody who's been a victim (of identity theft)."

-Edmund Mierzwinski

Why would a thief break into a secure home when all they really need to do is go through your mail box, garbage, or just locate your name in the phone book or on the internet? Today's identity thief is one step ahead of yesterday's laws that are not equipped to punish today's technology-savvy criminal.

Unfortunately, authorities simply do not possess the resources needed to adequately pursue identify theft as vigorously as more intrusive crimes like, say…burglary. And while a thief may be apprehended while breaking into your home, they will not be held for going through your mailbox (at least nowhere near as seriously). As stated above, our modern-day criminal is one step ahead of our legal system, and identity theft can be every bit as intrusive as burglary. All said, while our current laws offer limited or no protection against identity theft, there are measures that you can take to safeguard your identity. Let's explore them together.

Of Debits and Credits…

Debit and credit cards are, increasingly, the preferred payment method for transactions big and small. Knowing the rules as they apply to your bank and the type of account that you have is a critical component to protecting yourself. Be "in the know" when it comes to the rules of the road regarding each of your accounts.

Best Practice: *Favor the use your credit card over your debit card for regular monthly purchases and pay it off in full at the end of each month. Monitor your ratio of 'used' versus 'available' credit, keeping the ratio at 30% where possible. This will have the dual effect of both protecting you from ID theft, while maximizing your credit score.*

Many banks require that you argue a fraudulent debit card transaction within seventy-two hours in order to get reimbursed. This window extends to thirty days for credit card transactions. Using your credit card for common purchases, then paying it off monthly is a best practice that will give you the opportunity to receive and scrutinize your monthly statement; then report any fraudulent activity that may have occurred.

Using a credit card statement for all transactions makes good *risk management* sense.

Paying your card completely off at the end of each month (to maintain availability for the next month, while not incurring unwanted debt) makes good *financial* sense, as it will minimize finance charges.

Regularly monitoring used versus available credit on your account makes good *credit* sense, as it will assist you in keeping your credit score as high and as healthy as it can be *(as an added benefit, trying doing this with a rewards-based or affinity credit card*).

Maintain minimal balances in accounts that are attached to your debit card, and keep the majority of cash in your savings account as an added precaution. This strategy removes the majority of your liquid cash from the front lines while adding a layer of complexity to any would-be thief attempting to access your cash or identity. This is just an added strategy to aid in your overall risk management approach to protecting yourself and your assets.

Now let's talk about other areas of identity theft. Did you know that:

To obtain your address, today's modern day thief need only perform a reverse lookup of your phone number? (Your physical safety can be at risk as well as your identity.)

To obtain your social security number, today's modern day thief need only input your name, using an incorrect social security number, into a software program that will spit out your correct information (after displaying an error message with the original 'incorrect' information). Voila! Your social security number, on a silver platter.

To obtain your credit report, today's modern day thief need only use your name and address. As you know, the personal credit report is the golden gateway to a smorgasbord of personal information, including, but not limited to: current and past addresses, previous employers, credit card information, and more!

The modern-day, technology-enabled thief in each of the above cases, need not be a thief at all. It can be anyone on the street, including (and most likely) an overly aggressive marketing company.

Why – you ask? Because while using the above information for nefarious purposes may be illegal, simply obtaining it is not illegal. This is a grey area at best. Unfortunately, a surprising percentage of ID thieves are friends, family, and those that enter your home, like the cleaning lady.

In three simple steps a would-be thief (or aggressive marketing company) could have you name, address, phone number, social security number, and credit report. It sort of reminds me of the children's show, "Agent Oso", where Agent Oso solves problems in three special steps. I now picture my three year old pulling up social security numbers and credit reports in three special steps (in between watching Elmo and playing with his Thomas trains, of course). Life isn't quite that simple for ordinary honest folks; why should pulling your private information be made so simple for the dishonest and for corporations to obtain?

> ***Best Practice:*** *For roughly $20 per month, obtain a PO Box or the like (UPS Store, etc.) for all your bank and credit card statements, and phone or utility bills. This is an excellent risk-management practice against the intrusive forces of the universe. This also provides a personal security safeguard against would-be stalkers that may overhear you giving out your phone number (think, "reverse lookup"). The author of this chapter has maintained a personal UPS Store address, for this very purpose, for over ten years now.*

Other things you can do...

Shred! I know everyone should have heard this one by now, but it should not go unmentioned: Shred, shred (and shred!). Shred everything that you put into the garbage that has any personal or account information. Did you receive an offer of credit, membership, CD or DVD or book of the month club in the mail? They contain personal information. Shred them! Also, a word of advice: Rather than to discontinue shredding due to your fifth paper jam in twenty minutes, all because you saved money by purchasing the cheap shredder, do yourself a favor – Get the good model shredder! Putting a premium on your personal information and safety by investing in a good shredder will save you aggravation, especially when the paper jams. So invest in a good shredder, it will be well worth it in the long run. Remember — recovering from ID theft is a long, drawn-out process, which can cost thousands of dollars.

When shopping on the Internet look for the "s" added to the "http" in the URL address that you are making a purchase transaction in. The "https" signifies that you are now on a secure website.

Use a credit card for online purchases. Credit disputes are much easier than debit disputes. In a credit dispute, you are only liable up to $25 for a fraudulent transaction.

Have homeowners or renters insurance? Throw a rider on the policy to cover identity theft! It's very cheap and well worth the investment. And remember – know thy policy! (this to be explained in the chapter on Insurance).

With the above suggestions and tips your saftey, finances and sanity will be safeguarded.

THE BASICS: How & Why to Have Good Credit

by Vivian Gaspar

"The most important thing... is to establish credit - a reputation and character."

- John D. Rockefeller

Identity theft and credit usually go hand in hand. Being knowledgeable about your credit can go a long way in protecting both your identity and your credit. Outlined below are some fast facts that consumers should know about their credit and why it is important to maintain it.

Contrary to what many people think, it is possible to obtain a mortgage with a bankruptcy on your credit. The average time is two years after a bankruptcy is discharged (for most lenders).

Foreclosure is far worse than a bankruptcy in the world of mortgage credit. You are better off selling your home to an investor on one of those signs you see around town than you are to have your home foreclosed upon. You know – the ones that read: "We Buy Houses".

Opting to "short sale" your home will be better for your credit as well as your risk exposure. Please see a recommended real estate attorney. Just breaking even on your liens or taking a small loss is far better than allowing your home to go into foreclosure. There are also potential tax exposure risks possible (IRS) with a foreclosure which is why, for a variety of reasons; a "short sale" is much more advantageous.

The primary qualifier in selling your home in a short sale is if you are "underwater" on your mortgage (owing more than the value of your home).

If you are selling your home because you can no longer afford it please try to modify the payment. You should only sell your home if you no longer want to live it or are unable to maintain it. In my experiences (over 200 clients) the average home owner saves $500-$1,100 a month for 60 months. Then after the 60 months the payment gradually raises by 1% a year until you are back to your current interest rate which can mean you are modified for a total of 8-10 years for the average modification recipient.

Mortgage companies (and creditors in general) only consider your payments late in increments of: 30, 60, 90, 120 & 150 days. Even though you will incur a late charge after fifteen days late, mortgage lenders and other creditors have their own late fee schedules. In other words, you are only late after the 30th day. If you go to 29 days, it will not show up on your credit report even though you will have been charged a late fee and perhaps received collections calls. A late mortgage payment is taken the more seriously than most other late payments on your credit report, such as credit cards or car payments or other installment loans.

Another factor in your credit score and health is the length of time that the account has been open. All things equal, an account with the most (positive) history is viewed more favorably than an account that has been open for a shorter time period. Closing an account is usually viewed as a negative.

A very important aspect of your total credit rating is the ratio of available credit, meaning: the ratio of used versus unused credit on one card. Also, the ratio of available credit as it is compared to what is available on all of your accounts, together. Maintaining a thirty percent ratio is best. It is also best to have a mix of differing types of credit such as installment loans i.e.: an auto loan, and not just credit cards.

Having too many credit accounts is viewed negatively. The optimal number of credit card accounts is usually three to five open (major) credit cards. Unfortunately people are also judged negatively on types of credit cards, it is not seen favorably to have many individual store cards. (This would include gas stations and catalogs.) So when store clerks ask you if you want to save 10% on today's order by opening a store credit card, please think about your credit health before saying, "Sure."

It is also really recommended to review your credit card statement(s) each month for accuracy, making sure that transactions were really authorized by you and that your interest rate hasn't jumped up unexpectedly. Identity theft is easiest to get away with in small dollar amounts on a repeated basis so as not to alarm the card holder. For example you won't realize it if $29.99 is charged every month on a credit card as easily as if the amount is $299.00. When identity thieves do this low dollar amount theft to thousands of people on a monthly basis, it really is a very profitable scam for them. Remember, even though it might not be fair, you will be judged on your credit score and the contents of your actual credit report in everything from your auto and home-owner's insurance rates to background checks when you apply for a job. Protecting your credit is really more critical than most people realize, especially when that job you have been praying for is on the line.

Vivian Gaspar

As the Public Relations Director for an attorney specializing in mortgage modification, Vivian Gaspar has helped over 200 families to stay in their homes, by obtaining a mortgage modification which dramatically reduced monthly payments by 5-9 years or even, in come cases, for the balance of the loan. There were several clients which were aided in avoiding imminent foreclosure altogether. Ms. Gaspar had also been a recruiter, mortgage originator and a real estate agent. As a prior business owner she had been interviewed on television, newspaper and radio. Her business experience has helped her in advising her mortgage modification clients in their hardships.

Ms. Gaspar has been the founder and owner/operator of several businesses over the last 25 years. She has also been a public speaker on topics ranging from ID Theft to Mortgage Facts For Everyone. As someone who has worked individually with over 200 families in financial crisis in the last two years (as the Public Relations Director & Mortgage Modification Specialist in the legal office of V. James Castiglia in New Jersey) she heard similar stories and gave the same advice to people repeatedly. Her experiences have ranged from owning a marketing company to being a recruiter to being a mortgage loan officer which helped her in deciphering people's current mortgages as the first step in Mortgage Modification consultations. During the mortgage modification appointments she always started off by reviewing the client's origination documents to ensure that they had been fully aware of the specifics of their current mortgage. Unfortunately, Ms. Gaspar had found that over half of her modification clientele had been misled by the loan officer who placed those clients into the mortgage that currently needed modification.

Part of her responsibilities as Mr. Castiglia's Public Relations Director was to give speeches at civic organizations such as the Lions Club and Rotary Club. After several of these speeches, Ms. Gaspar had been approached with the suggestion to spread her knowledge to a wider audience and to consider writing a book. In February of 2010, she started giving the idea of writing a book on mortgage modification and the foreclosure process more serious consideration. Over the next few months Ms. Gaspar had concluded that she could help a wider base of people in crisis if she covered a broad subject base.

Ms. Gaspar started an outline of chapters on topics she wanted to see included in the book. Immediately she thought of all the business contacts she had accumulated over her years of attending business networking events, including those she organized and hosted. She was the founding member of the only lunch time Le Tip on the East Coast at that time and founded her own location of Network Plus where the meetings were held every week for over a year. Ms. Gaspar had met several of the contributing authors at events which she hosted in 2009 and 2010 in Morris County, New Jersey. It was the knowledge of these seasoned professionals that Ms. Gaspar wanted to bring to the general public. These topics had been created and outlined by Ms. Gaspar and included the expertise of 28 experts on 38 topics.

Ms. Gaspar's first book, "How to Survive Your Financial Crisis", was released in February 2011 with the Spanish translation set to release in the Summer of 2012 along with a second edition as well as that edition's Spanish version to be released within 90 days thereafter.

Ms. Gaspar also envisions the translation of both editions into the top 10 languages spoken throughout the world, with international sales and marketing through the website: www.howtosurviveyourfinancialcrisis.com.

Debt Settlement

by Rocco Sileo

"Neither a borrower nor a lender be."
- William Shakespeare

Have you ever fallen behind on a loan or interest payment? Who hasn't, right? Well, the focus of this chapter is to educate you the consumer about credit cards and the companies that issue them.

Did you know that it would take an individual, making minimum payments, fifty eight years to pay off a $10,000 credit card, assuming a 19% APR? In the end, the individual would have paid almost $29,000 in interest payments alone! As of the time of this writing I see many people that pay 30% APR's. There is even a bank that offers credit cards in the 50%-70% APR range!

Understand, the goal of the credit card company is to get you the consumer on a non-stop payment treadmill that directs your cash into their pockets. The name of the game is cash-flow, and the math goes something like this: What is the highest payment that a consumer (given their profile) can afford to make, leaving no discretionary cash behind? You see, in the bank's eyes, your discretionary cash represents money that is left on the table, and they want it. There is a line beyond which you the consumer can no longer afford to make payment to the bank. The banks business model is built to bring you as close to this point as possible and to keep you there as long as possible. Credit-math is optimized for this, and you stand no chance of winning. It's like walking into a casino: The house always wins!

A perfect storm of circumstances can push anyone over the edge. Circumstances which may include sickness, a loss of job, or decrease in household income could easily push a seemingly affordable debt-load past the point of affordability. At this point we start to consider our options. To many people, the only option appears to be the dreaded word bankruptcy. One of the main goals of this chapter is educate you the consumer that you have options other than bankruptcy. One of these options is Debt Settlement. Debt settlement has flown under the radar of consumers for a long time, but in recent years has picked up considerable steam. Previously, debt settlement was only available to consumers that took the time to research all their options. As it turns out, most creditors are willing to significantly reduce outstanding debt balances if a consumer is struggling. In some cases as of late, there have been consumers that were able to settle their debt for as little as ten to fifteen cents on the dollar!

Nowadays, you can hire a professional law firm to assist in this process. By using a law firm, the reduced amount may be paid back over time (usually three or four years). The consumer's monthly outlay is often times half the usual monthly interest expense. The point is that a person can get a cheaper payment to get out of debt as compared to what it currently costs to stay in debt.

The logical question is: "What's the catch"? Simply put, a consumer must be struggling in order to get help. This is not going to work for those with assets. In fact, the net worth of a consumer may have a negative impact on taxable income for forgiven debt; so be sure to confirm with your accountant as well, when considering this option.

Also, a consumer must be either unable or unwilling to continue making the minimum payments. An example of unwilling may be someone on a fixed income with no disposable income left over after the interest on the credit cards are paid.

Yes, this will lead to late marks on credit reports and possible judgment filings as public records in some cases, but is it really all that bad, considering the alternative?

First, most candidates for debt settlement do not have strong credit to begin with and when only minimum payments are made each month, regardless of pay history, the credit score will go down a little further leading to the slow death of a credit rating. A judgment will prevent the consumer from having clean title until the account is settled. So as long as there are no major purchases or sales needed to be made until after the accounts are settled, it shouldn't be a huge factor in the decision making process.

Compared to bankruptcy, a debt settlement plan has far less long term ramifications. Through the settlement process, a typical consumer will have a few late payments that turned into collections or judgments and were eventually paid. Settled accounts are easier to remove from a credit report and have less of an impact on a consumer's score than a bankruptcy. The example below offers three different options available to a consumer that is struggling with credit card debt and looking for a solution.

John and Mary have $10,000 in credit card debt with a 19% interest rate. They live paycheck to paycheck, and after all living expenses are paid, they can only afford to make the minimum payment of $350 each month. What options are available to them?

a) Continue to make the minimum payments for the next three years and hope things eventually pick up. This option would cost $12,000 in interest payments and the balance would still be $10,000 owed at the end of three years.

b) Find the up-front money to file bankruptcy. This option may cost a couple thousand dollars, just to hire the attorney, in some states. Then, just hope that there is no forced repayment of any kind, and that the public record never prevents the consumer from getting a job or in some cases effect professional licensing. Also, realize that it will take a long time for

c) the public record to come off the credit report. See the chapter by a bankruptcy attorney in this book.

d) Enter into a settlement plan to repay approximately $5,000 total spread out over three years ($138 per month). Deal with short term credit ramifications and have disposable income left over at the end of the month to establish savings.

Settling for less is not always the best route to take. Knowledge is power! The more information you have at your disposal, the better. It will lead to better and more informed decision making. Debt settlement has undergone recent regulatory changes, and there has been plenty scrutiny in the industry as of late. Much of the bad press has been due to both, propaganda from the credit card companies, as well as, a few bad players in the industry that misled consumers.

The advice is for consumers to do their homework; take stock of their personal circumstances, and on the company or law firm they are considering for debt settlement. Find out the fees and when they are taken before signing a contract. The option to negotiate on your own is always available if someone has the time and knows what they are doing.

As of the time of the writing of this chapter and book, our country is facing the worst economic climate since the Great Depression. There are literally thousands upon thousands of consumers who have made the tough choice to get help now, so that they may move on with their lives. This has worked to the advantage of consumers, as creditors have had no choice but to react with leniency. For those that are on the fence, do not wait until it is too late. Eventually the worst will pass and creditors may not be so willing to forgive debts as much as they are today. Stay positive, and remember — You are your own best asset.

Rocco Sileo

Rocco has been involved in the financial services industry for over a decade. His professional career began as a mortgage broker where he originally focused his energies on the education of homeownership benefits. After passing the NJ State Banker Exam, he was a partner in a successful mortgage company for several years before taking a serious interest in the industry of debt settlement and negotiation. In 2006, after hours of research and testing, he officially began a new business to fill the much needed void for consumers who were looking for help with their unsecured debts. Since then, Rocco served briefly on the Board at Large of T.A.S.C. (The Association Of Settlement Companies); which was an industry trade group devoted to consumer awareness of best practices for debt settlement and has recently expanded his business to form a processing center on behalf of different law firms who have been retained to assist consumers negotiate debt. If you would like to speak with Rocco personally, please feel free to use the contact information below

Rocco Sileo
rocco.legalprotection@gmail.com

SECTION 2

Practical Help For The Unemployed

Lost Your Job?
Understand Your COBRA Benefits

by Harry Herbst

When an employee involuntarily loses their health benefit due to being laid off or fired, they are entitled to COBRA benefits, which are federally mandated. Employees are eligible for COBRA benefits for 15 months in the state of New Jersey. The employer cannot prevent the employee from signing up and participating in COBRA. Unfortunately the employee is responsible for the entire premium. The Obama administration did not renew the American Reinvestment and Recovery Act or (ARRA) as of this writing. There is discussion but no legislation to reinstate ARRA at this time. (May 2011) This is causing a tremendous burden on any terminated employee. What I hear, as a practitioner, on a daily basis is that an employee could barely afford the medical insurance while they were employed and now that they are unemployed it is not in the realm of reality. If the newly unemployed individual has children under the age of eighteen, they can apply for a program called NJ Kids Care which is a government subsidized program. (please see your state's equivalent if outside New Jersey.) Depending on assets and any income (i.e. severance packages, unemployment benefits, pensions) from their previous employer, the cost could be zero to a fraction of what private insurance premiums would consist of. Under extreme circumstances, Medicaid for individuals and families over the age of eighteen can be applied for as well.

As a result, in this crisis we are facing there are many new uninsured individuals. I cannot state with enough emphasis the hardships this has caused. When an unemployed person contacts my office, because the COBRA rate is excessive, the only remedy that I have as an independent health insurance producer is an individual policy. Individual insurance is different from group insurance in that the carrier sets the rates for individual health policies whereas with group health insurance there are several rating factors. The benefits are very limited for individual health insurance, for example: prescription benefits are covered at 50%. If someone has a pre-existing condition and is on several mediations it can get very expensive at a 50% responsibility which is all that the insurance carrier will cover. In addition, deductibles and coinsurance are in many cases significantly higher than their previous insurance coverage. This leaves the individual facing higher out of pocket expenses for Lab Testing, emergency rooms, and hospital visits. Please bear in mind that an individual cannot be uninsured for more than 90 days (3 months) or they are subject to a pre-existing conditions clause. This means that there will be no medical coverage for 6 months on a group policy and 12 months on an individual policy. A pre-existing condition is defined as any condition you are currently being treated for. For example: High Blood pressure. That condition along with any medication you were taking would not be covered on the insurance for either 6 months or 12 months depending on the policy.

An exception to the COBRA/ARRA rules is for a Survivor Benefit. When a dependent loses their health insurance because a spouse dies, they may remain on COBRA for thirty-six months or three years. These rules apply to someone who is employed in the state of New Jersey, as COBRA rules vary from state to state. If a company closes their doors or goes out of business, all those who have lost their jobs as a result of this, and any former employees previously covered under COBRA will lose their benefits. Under COBRA law, if there is no business, there are no COBRA benefits.

As a general rule, employers detest COBRA benefits because they don't want to have to collect the premiums from the former employees. If an employee misses a payment or doesn't remit the premium in a timely manner, then the employer has the right to terminate the employee from COBRA and the employee cannot get back onto COBRA once they have been terminated. Many employers will hire a Third Party Administrator, or "TPA", that will handle the collection of premium dollars and overall administration, maintenance, and reporting that the company would normally have with COBRA participants. It takes the stress of chasing after a former employee off of the employer and makes the COBRA process a lot smoother.

Harry Herbst

Mr. Herbst is a licensed insurance agent who started in 1975. He started his own Insurance Agency in 2002 working with small business owners in small employee benefits arena. Mr. Herbst is a member of the National Association of Insurance agents and Financial Advisors NAIFA. He is also a member of the National Association of Health Underwriter NAHU and was awarded a membership to the prestigious Million Dollar Round Table (MDRT.)

Mr. Herbst also proudly served his country as a US Navy Veteran. He is also Senior Vice Commander of the Jewish War Veterans and a Trustee of Freehold Jewish Center. Active in the various Networking Associations and Chambers of Commerce.

Mr. Herbst holds a BA from the City University of New York and has an MA from the New School for Social Research.

HARRY HERBST & ASSOCIATES
Insurance & Financial Planning
708 Ginesi Drive
Suite 206
Morganville, NJ 07751
(732) 536-5200
(732) 536-5201 (Fax)
1-888-786-5201 (toll free)

How To Get Your Recruiter To Focus On You

by Joanne Lucas

I'm a recruiter and I want your attention!

I have been a recruiter since before fax machines, which means that I have spoken with many candidates as well as employers.

My job is to help employers attract and retain outstanding candidates in the Administrative, Finance, Sales, Customer Service, IT as well as office arenas. I do that by finding people and by having people find me for the opportunities that I'm working on as well as the ones that I can create by marketing the experience of a candidate to an employer that I know can use that experience.

Although times have changed with the Job Boards and Social Networking, I still get referrals and ask for people with similar experience to people who they know can do a job.

How do you stand out? Have a resume that states what you have done and how you've helped. Return phone calls. Give information and take and use information to help you get the job that you desire.

And please be aware of your e-mail address -- that can be the first thing that people think about you. Be professional and simple. Do not use e-mail addresses with cute phrases and nicknames.

When you call me about an opportunity, please be prepared to speak about it. The job number doesn't help me. I understand that you're flexible, but be prepared to tell me how your background fits the opportunity.

Please apply for the jobs that you can DO! I know that you're a quick learner, but offices are so lean today, that they need someone who can hit the ground running. Also, do your homework. Find out about our company and the people that we usually work with. In other words, do your homework. Show me that you will research my client and that you are prepared to make a change.

When is the best time to get to know a recruiter? When you don't need one. It's like banks that only like to lend you money when you don't really need it. When a recruiter calls to tell you about a great opportunity and asks who you know that is qualified for that position, talk with him/her. If you do know people, refer them. You will be doing a friend a good turn. If it sounds like an opportunity that is interesting to you, be available to spend time with the recruiter as well as the employer. You may not be able to talk at work. We understand that. But we DO need to talk.

A friend may have heard about future layoffs, or may not have received the promotion promised, or not received the raise that was expected. Your friend may not tell anyone due to either embarrassment or thinking that no one can help. By introducing your friend to a recruiter, you will be doing your friend a service – if not for now, but for the future when knowing a recruiter is important.

A lot of people are happy where they are (we all know unhappy people... taking that unhappiness away will REALLY make them unhappy). A great candidate is someone who is happy in his/her job, but if a great opportunity were to come up would take it and start with two weeks notice. That is the candidate that I like to work with.

Get to know and trust the recruiter. Know that when he/she calls, there is something important to discuss... if not now, but some time in the future. I've spoken with candidates who tell me that they don't need a recruiter. But, then the impossible happens and they don't have any place to turn.

OK. Now that you have a recruiter that you trust and that there is an opportunity that sounds interesting... now what?

Be a part of our team. Make it easy for us to get to know you. Give us the information that we need to be able to present you to our client. We are on your side! Our client is the company – the company pays our fee, but unless you're happy, it's not going to work.

We give you all the information that we have about the company, the particular hiring authority and what, in particular, they're looking for in their new employee. We're doing that so that you will do well on your interview. If we suggest a particular part of your experience to focus on, then please focus on that part. We know that you get nervous, but we're doing the best that we can do to help you do well on the interview and get the new opportunity.

If a resume needs to be "tweaked", please do it. We will never ask you to state that you did something that you didn't do, but will ask you to add what you have done. That piece of information may help an employer decide to hire you.

We will talk about Counter Offer with you. Please read up on whether taking one is a good idea. When a candidate comes to me and says that everything about a current position is perfect except for... before I work with him/her, I recommend that he/she go to the employer and see what can be done to fix the problem.

Of course, there is no mention of leaving, or that if the problem isn't fixed, you will leave... that may help the "leaving" happen before you want it. But, if you feel you need a raise, bring in the numbers that you have to show how your work has helped the company. Have you increased efficiency? Created a new way to process orders? Worked with customers who were unhappy and solved the problems to keep the client? Employers give raises because they need you, not because you need one.

After that, if the employer cannot fix the problem, we can work together. My job isn't to get you a raise unless it's with my client. I don't want to waste anyone's time with a candidate who really doesn't want to change jobs or doesn't want to work. Of course, if you do get a raise with your current employer, that's great for all... you got what you want, the employer keeps an excellent candidate, and I haven't wasted anyone's time.

Please tell me any situations that may come up that would keep you from accepting and starting a job... vacations, other offers, time to be vested, bonuses and profit sharing. Surprises don't work well with us.

On an interview, your job is to get the job, not decide if you want it. Do your homework. Come prepared with answers to questions that you will be asked as well as questions for you to ask the hiring authority. Research the company; research the industry and competitors. Know what is happening in the business to know how your experience will best help the company.

Practice answering the questions. One question that people don't like is the "Tell me about yourself" question. How do you answer that? It is NOT personal. Remember it's like a trial... your lawyer will only ask what the opposing attorney can question. A company shouldn't ask about children, but, once you bring them up, the topic is fair game.

The answer to that should be, "This is what I've done, and this is how I've helped. How can I help you?" The interviewer will give you the main points that are required, and you can tell him/her how you can do it. Is there anything easier than that? That is also the "elevator speech" that everyone should have. That 60 second introduction should be an introduction that leads to questions and interest.

When asked if you have any questions, the answer should be in two parts: 1) "I saw on your website that... ." Hit them on the head that you did your homework. 2) Assume that the job is yours, "When I do this... who will get the results? What is my main goal in the first 90 days?"

An interview is a sales opportunity. You MUST ask for the job. "I'd like to work here, what's the next step?" And... just sit there and smile. Don't add anything until the interviewer says something.

The last questions will get you quite a bit of information. Ask: "What do you consider my strengths and weaknesses?" That is a win-win for you. If the interviewer can't think of any weaknesses, then ask for the opportunity again. I'm glad to hear that. I'd like to work here. What's our next step?" If there is a weakness, at least you have an opportunity to overcome it. Not knowing about it doesn't make it go away.

After the interview, call me as soon as you leave the interview. I can't talk with the employer until I speak with you. I can only believe that you're not interested if I don't hear from you.

You may not get the offer for the job, but if you work with the recruiter, you will get another chance. Make the recruiter look foolish for sending you, and that will be the only interview that you're sent on.

We also stay in touch after you start. We love good news... so please let us know when you really like your new job. We also need to know if there are problems. But, PLEASE don't call us when you know that we won't be there, and PLEASE don't email us bad news. We can work with you through problems, but we need to TALK. I can't help you unless I know the problem and can help find a solution. "No news is good news" is NOT the way to start a new job or the way to work with a professional recruiter.

Remember us when others that you know are either looking to hire or change jobs. If we've helped you, please let others know.

How to work with a recruiter? Work WITH us and the result will be positive!

How To Ace Your Next Job Interview

by Joanne Lucas

So, when does your interview start? Is it when you meet the employer? Is it when you set the appointment? Or, is it when you apply on line?

Your interview starts when your future employer or recruiter sees your information for the first time. It can be your resume, Facebook page, LinkedIn profile, or other public information. Whatever the source, you want to represent yourself well to future employers.

Let's start with your resume. Check your e-mail address. It should be: FirstName.LastName2011@abcxyz.com. Check that your e-mail represents yourself professionally. Keep your personal one (although future employers can see that one on your social sites), and get a free one with your name. That way, you will know when you have business e-mails and you will present yourself as a future employee.

The same goes for the message on your phone. When I call, I don't want to hear music, I don't want a "message", I just want to leave a message. One theme throughout this will be to make it easy for the person who may hire you. I understand that your child is cute. Save the message and re-install it after you get a job. And, if there is someone at your home who can't take messages accurately, please ask them to let all calls go to answering machines. That way, you will get the message accurately. I have been hung up on many times because the person answering the call can't take a message. You'll never know how many interviews you've missed.

Have paper and a writing utensil near the phone. Answer calls professionally. Be ready to interview. When you're looking for a job, your job is getting a job. So, when an employer calls to set up a meeting, be prepared to offer, "today or tomorrow." If people tell me that they can come in next week, I ask them to call then. I know that they won't and I have just saved time.

Dressing appropriately is important. You want the interviewer to remember what you can do, not what you wore! That means not a lot of cologne, nothing short, tight or low cut. And, shoes shined, shirt pressed and wearing a suit that fits. Limit jewelry to one or two pieces. Keep your interview outfit ready at all times. No one will know that you wore it the previous day.

When you go to the interview, show up 15 minutes before your interview time. Go alone! If someone needs to drive you, let that person stay in the car. Unless an ambulance comes for you, the longer you're there, the better it is.

Make friends with the Gatekeeper. That may be the receptionist or administrative assistant. Have some small talk ready. Have your smile ready. You will be amazed at how many people have lost jobs because they had an attitude with the Gatekeeper. That person will be on the phone as you're on the way to meet the interviewer. That information will either get you a long or short interview.

In the same vein, if asked to fill out an application, fill it out. Writing "See resume" will only show that you're not following directions and that you take short cuts. The application will have the exact dates, to whom you reported, salary and reason for leaving... all very important information to the target company. Please know that the application is a legal document. Be sure that your information is correct. Also, remember: Your favorite four letter word is "Open." Use it when asked for salary. You will write your previous salary, so they will know where you fit in their salary range.

If you were earning more and are willing to take a cut in salary to work for this company, be prepared to overcome that objection. Companies have hired candidates who have taken a cut, been trained, and then left to take their previous salary. It is very expensive for a company, both in actual costs, as well as morale, so they need to be as sure as possible that it won't happen again.

Also, bring reference information. Your company closed. Does that mean that you have no references at all? Do your homework. Find people who worked with you. Written letters are OK, but how many times have you heard, "You write the letter, and I'll sign it". Phone numbers or e-mail addresses show that you have prepared for the interview.

Speaking of preparing, with today's internet, there is no excuse to have no information about the company and the industry that it's in. Be sure to have questions to ask. You may write them down (it shows that you prepared). One of the worst things you can do is to have no questions.

One of the questions you may hear is, "Tell me about yourself." The interviewer doesn't want to know personal information. He/she wants to know how hiring you is going to help the company. Have your "elevator speech" ready. This is what I've done, this is how I've helped, how can I help you?" At this point, you will hear what the responsibilities are and you can tell that person how you can do that and help the company at the same time.

If you're asked if you have any questions, answer in two ways: 1) I saw on your website that... or when I Googled your business... I found that... how will that relate to my responsibilities? 2) Ask questions as if you have the job... what will be the composition of the team that I will be on... where will I get the information on new products or services?

The interview is a sales opportunity, and the sale doesn't happen unless asked for. So smile, lean forward and tell the interviewer that you'd like to work there, and ask what the next step is. An employer wants to hire someone who wants to work there. This is a time to be positive. That doesn't mean saying that you're staying until you get an offer. When asking for the job, you have a great chance. If you say you're not leaving until hired, they call security.

If you're asked "illegal questions," what do you do? If you think about it, the only thing that the employer wants to know is if you're going to be there. Answer their concern. Go through the interview. Then assess if it is a place where you want to work. You still have control of your future. The company may be naïve as to questions that may be asked, or they can be a place to run from. But, without going through the entire interview, you won't be able to make that decision.

If asked about salary, the best way to answer it is to do your homework, and know what the salary is for that opportunity in your part of the country. "I'm looking for a good opportunity. I know you'll be fair." They will have seen what you were making in your last position and unless you were grossly underpaid or if you're taking a pay cut, they will continue when your salary is within their range.

If offered the job on the interview and you want it, TAKE IT! If you're not sure, just say that it sounds like a good opportunity and you'd like to think about it overnight. You'll know on the way home if it's the job for you. Two weeks only lets the employer know that you will take the job if nothing better comes up. No one likes to be second best. It's not a good way to start a job.

If you're looking for more money, plan your conversation for the next day. State what you're looking for and be sure to explain how you will benefit the company. Know that your salary has to fit in with the department. An extra $5,000 may mean a raise for the others in the department (people DO find out), and that may not be in the budget.

Give them a way to give you a raise if you meet certain guidelines. "If I can bring in the project in three months and under budget, can we discuss a bonus or a raise?" Many times that can be a positive because you will be bringing a value to the company. However, be prepared to either accept the job or turn it down at that time based on that conversation.

Send two kinds of Thank You notes. An e-mail thank you is great for instant gratification. A hand written snail mail will show your follow up skills. If it's between two people and you send the note, you have a good chance of getting the offer. All business is based on follow up. If you show that before you're hired, it's a good indication of future performance.

When you start a new job, make friends with people who LIKE working there. You can always find malcontents, but why do that? I'm sure that even at Microsoft there are unhappy people. As my husband says, "You need to be happy 10 minutes a day. Five minutes on the way to work and five minutes on the way home." If you can do that, you have it made and you have taken the next step in your career.

Joanne Lucas

Joanne Lucas Manager of Staffing, Winston Staffing, Rutherford, NJ

Ms. Lucas has been a recruiter for over 25 years. She started before fax machines were even a figment of someone's imagination and now job seekers wouldn't think of working without the internet!

Ms. Lucas is on advisory boards of post high school educational facilities where she helps place their students as well as help prepare them for interviews and the workplace. Ms. Lucas has helped interview students who are applying for scholarships and worked to recommend the winners.

Ms. Lucas especially likes helping candidates take the next step in their careers. She helps determine the social and educational life of the people that we work with as well as help our clients grow their businesses.

Ms. Lucas specializes in Education and Real Estate, but also work with opportunities in the Administrative areas.

Ms. Lucas is married to John De Silva, and has a daughter Suzie, in Arizona, who is married and is a music teacher on an Indian Reservation.

Joanne Lucas
Manager of Staffing
301 Route 17 North
Rutherford, NJ 07070
201-460-9200x204
joannelucas2001@yahoo.com.
www. winstonstaffing.com

Can't Find a Job?
Direct Marketing - A Real Income Alternative

by Camille Re

"You can have everything you want in life if you help enough people get what they want."

-Zig Zigler

A legitimate and viable home-based business solution that is frequently overlooked is Network Marketing, commonly referred to as Multi-Level Marketing, or "MLM" for short. Network Marketing has received its fair share of negative press over the years; however, one would be hard-pressed to find an alternative with a lower cost and as low an overhead as an MLM. The role of the MLM deserves special mention in this book.

The first MLM started back in the 1950's with Amway. Amway was the first company to put together an MLM compensation framework. After Amway came other MLM entities replete with their own variation of the MLM model. Examples of these include; Mary Kay Cosmetics, Avon, Pampered Chef, Lia Sophia, Tastefully Simple, and the list goes on. Many people have made successful careers from these companies while others have made just extra part-time income depending, of course, on how you build and market their system. I have been a distributor for a few of these organizations in the past as my children were growing up, so I am familiar with different compensation plans, what to look for and questions to ask. Over the past 25 years I have never given up on my belief in the power of building a home based business. Home based businesses give you time, freedom, and part- or full-time hours, with minimal start-up costs, potential tax advantages, and little downside. Additionally, the possibility to earn a residual six figure income is very realistic, with the right effort of course.

When you join an MLM you have the opportunity to not only make money from the products that you sell but from the sales of other representatives – the people below you – your downline. The person above you who signed your up is your direct upline.

When performing research on a potential MLM company, do not rely on pumping the company name into Google or other search engines. You will immediately reach the search result entitled, "Scam". MLM's are not scams, so please do not let someone else's failure dictate your future success or failure. Do not rely on non-credible sources for your research. Perform research but make sure that it is fair and unbiased. A good research tool is the company's own financial report. See how long they've been in business and how many quarters of growth they have.

Good advice would be to see what you are getting for your start-up. Know the risks. Do they take back products? What training and support can you expect? Set expectations with your upline. Find a company that will work with you, teach you and have a good return policy with little risk.

Some characteristics to look for when deciding on an MLM organization are as follows:

Apprentice Program

This is a program whereby you may join the company with no money down. Apprentices usually start out as commissioned sales reps, where the commissions are banked within the company until you are able to fully join. Apprenticeship organizations will provide training and work with you for up to one year to learn the business. Once you have enough money "banked", it is then transferred into your own distributorship account. Apprenticeship programs are great because they teach you how to generate customers and get trained even before you start your business. You now set yourself up for success from the start. Another way is to work with a distributor who will allow you to sell for her/him and put your commissions away until you have enough to start with the company.

A Legacy for Your Family

This is where your MLM distributorship is considered a willable asset. If you grow your business to six figures and life is good, that's great, but what if something happens to you? Can you will your business to your wife/husband or a third party? Ensuring the continuation of your business so that your family does not have to worry is a very good feeling. Always ask if the venture that you are entering into is willable.

Break Away

This is where the MLM company will actually "break away" one of the down-lines from your organization if that downline is building at a stronger pace or if they start to out-earn you. The MLM company may then take the downline from your organization and give you a much smaller portion of their business than if it was still part of your downline. For example, if you normally receive 30% from the production of a specific downline, you may receive 4% after they break away. Hmmm... all that training and effort and now you are awarded with a pay cut. It kind of makes you wonder whether your upline will train you adequately, or inadequately in fear of eventually losing business? Not all MLM's are created equal, and not all MLM's have a "break-away" clause in their contract. Look for this prior to signing up.

Training

It is critical to identify the level of training and support that you will receive from both the company and your immediate upline, as a new MLM distributor. Any training or assistance that the MLM company provides will be in writing and part of their business plan/model. This is a given. That said, do you expect the top dog to dedicate time and resources into training a new distributor that is seven levels down from him or her? Probably not. In this regard, it is best set expectations with your sponsor (your upline, the one that brought you into the business) as to the level of support that you may expect to receive from them. All training and support aside, it is up to YOU to come up to speed with what you need to in order to run a successful home-based MLM business. Read your manual. Work the program as instructed. Lucky for you, there is no reinventing of the wheel here.

Bonuses

This is a question that many never ask: Are there bonuses and how are they paid? First, all companies have bonuses, however, many do not understand how they are paid until they lose one. Get to know your bonus details! Many companies work by a point system. As your points grow higher, you may qualify for a bonus. In most cases from what I have seen, you need to reach your goal in a month's time. If you don't get the points or hit your goal in 30 days time, you lose your bonus. Education is key. You need to learn the company's bonus rules. I have seen so many people work so hard to reach a goal, just to miss it by one point, and all they get is a pat on the back and an "atah-boy, better luck next time". My advice is to look for bonuses that don't have a 30-day end time. Look for the longest end time, they are out there.

Gifting Points

As you place orders that have a point structure you earn bonuses. Many companies have a "Business Volume" or the like attached to each product. This is good and there are many companies that pay this way. Gifting points is a lot like sharing your volume. Ask if you can do this? Place an order and give the volume to the distributor at the bottom of your line. This way when the volume flows up… everyone can get a piece of the action. It's a really nice concept and helps to hold a team together. This will also aid in downline retention as it will decrease the percentage of people who quit.

Horizontal vs. Vertical Marketing

Everything discussed up to this point has been characteristic of Horizontal marketing. Vertical marketing, also referred to as "Binary" marketing provides an environment where everyone on a financial team has economic synergy. There are two organizations in vertical marketing where your team shares all commissions, and you get paid different percentages at various levels. What differentiates vertical from horizontal marketing is that only two organizations are required in vertical marketing, whereas six organizations is the average model in horizontal marketing. Why the number two? Because two is the smallest multiplier for the highest profits. One thing to know is that not all vertical organizations are considered MLM's (although most are). In vertical marketing you don't need to build as many teams. This makes life easier and provides the potential to make more money, while minimizing the (horizontal marketing) hassle of losing people in your downline. Be educated on the various percentages and how many levels down that you are compensated for. You want the highest percentage from your team for as many levels down as possible. Do your own research to ensure that the MLM company that you join is able to support its compensation model, or you might find yourself with an MLM that will go out of business.

MLM's work because they are backed up by a proven business model. The "trick", for lack of a better term, is to work the system as instructed. There is no reinventing the wheel.

All said, not all MLM's are created equal. It is less a matter of a good versus bad MLM, than it is in finding the one that's right for you. You will get out of your business what you put into it.

As a mother of four children (three of them with special needs), the flexibility of a home-based MLM business has great appeal to me. It was very hard for me to go out into the work force and find a job that would allow me to care for my children, take them to doctor appointments, hospitals or just take care of them without getting fired by a boss. Having a home-based business was the best option for me. I know a woman who had premature twins that weighed only one pound at birth. She spent months in the hospital with her two children with no worries as to where her next check was going to come from. She watched other moms cling to cell phones in futile attempts to convince their bosses to let them stay just a little longer. They had to leave their babies in the hands of doctors and nurses and hope that their children were still alive when they returned to the hospital from their jobs. Residual income is freedom to do what you want when you want with who you want. It's spending time with grandparents who are sick in the hospital while everyone else is stuck in an office. It's doing homework with your children at 3:00 in the afternoon or a family vacation that you can take whenever you want. You are your own boss, you eat when you want to eat, sleep until you are done, and tell yourself what you are worth.

One of my favorite questions that I get asked a lot is, "Do I have to sell?" The answer to this age-old (MLM) question is an emphatic "YES". Everyone is a salesperson. Whether you are selling a product or service, selling yourself to a potential employer or life partner, or selling your children on your beliefs; you are selling yourself each and every day of your life. When it comes to surviving your financial crisis, all options are on the table, and you shouldn't limit yourself or let any negative "I can't sell" thoughts creep into your psyche. Any business is work, and a home-based business is no exception. The hardest part is having the discipline to treat your home-based business like a business. Treat it like a million dollar business and it should pay you like one.

Camille Re

Camille Re was a hairdresser for 10 years and then retired to stay home with her children. She is Married and has 4 children, 3 girls and 1 boy. Two girls of her girls suffer from Junior Rheumatoid Arthritis and her son is diagnosed with Autism.

As a mother it was difficult for her to hold a job since she has several children with special needs. Mrs. Re's days were filled with doctor, hospital and therapists appointments. Since she has this very necessarily busy schedule Camille found herself looking for a home based business. This allows her to have the time and freedom to take care of her work and her family. Camille is her own boss and she makes her own hours.

Camille is an Independent Distributor of an internet marketing company called Market America Inc.

Camille's title is: Certified NutraMetrix Consultant. She is well versed at implementing a wellness programs through advanced supplements. However she is not limited to health and wellness products. Her partners within the organization work with: weight Management; Pet Care; Personal Care; Home and Garden; auto care; internet shopping; web design; debt Consolidation; Cosmetics; and music. She also works as a Non-Profit Consultant. Camille loves what she does because she can offer something for everyone and help so many people with their health as well as their finances. Camille especially loves that she is able to offer a 2-35% cash back program for all of her customers.

With Market America she is a multiple Local, District, and Regional challenge winner and is a member other North Jersey Leadership Association.

She now has an on going residual income and a business which is willable to her children.

Camille Re
www.CRcashback.com
optimalhealth.re@gmail.com
Contact number: 862-812-0639

How Anyone Can Make Money From Home

by Vivian Gaspar

Are you tired of crying, or just feeling like it, because there aren't any jobs to be had in your area or 500 people are applying for each job opening? Do you think the phrase "work from home" is just a scam or for anyone but you?

As someone who has found or created opportunities for myself to work from home for the last 15 years I know that working from home is for anyone who can force themselves to be focused. The saying "necessity is the mother of invention" is very true. Basically, if you need money badly enough, you WILL do what it takes to make an opportunity work and ignore other issues which can make it difficult for the average person to work from home.

You do not need an extra bedroom to use as a home office. For the people who say that they do not have a separate home office they are simply using an excuse instead of finding a solution to that obstacle. For many years I used either a part of my small living room for my "office" or just worked at my dining room table. If you have children have them play in their rooms or watch TV in another room.

The other most common obstacle is, "I just can't concentrate. My cluttered house or dirty dishes are just calling to me." For that, my solution is to make both a weekly and a daily task list which will get you to a goal. Then be extremely focused on each task and clearly mark off each task as they are completed. Also, use a reward system for yourself. For example, after doing two important tasks "reward" yourself with a five minute break of a snack or TV or even checking your Facebook status.

Now, that you have settled that you can be focused enough to work from home and where in your home you will work, what will you do?

The easiest way to work from home is telemarketing or cold calling. Anyone who has a phone and speaks clearly can train themselves to be an effective telemarketer. Forget the past negative experience you may have had with people pestering you at dinner time. Telemarketing is a very effective sales tool which generates billions of dollars in sales annually. I know you might be thinking that you do not want to be "one of THOSE bothersome people." However everyone who runs a small business needs more sales, and every salesperson regardless of who they work for or what they sell, would love qualified leads to call. The question to ask yourself is, "How badly do I need money and do I have the attitude that I am willing to do what it takes?" It has been estimated that 40% - 60% of a salesperson's time is spent generating leads so all sales professionals would love to have qualified leads handed to them. By using leads which are provided to them this makes any sales professional's income increase anywhere between 20-50% because they no longer need to take time to generate their own leads.

This is an occupation that you can easily do from home. Once you have proven yourself to be a reliable source you can easily get more work than you can handle and make anywhere from $8 to $20 per hour plus commission or bonus. Don't forget you now have tax savings as well by being able to write off your phone bill (or a portion thereof), a portion of your rent or mortgage and other related expenses. This is now your business and you now set the rules and no longer have to worry about being laid off again. Also, you do not need top set up a company. You can be billed as 1099. Ask your CPA which is best for you.

OK, you are willing to give it a try, but how do you get customers to pay you? Well, don't think that by looking in your local paper or classified section on the Internet you will find a company local to you. That might happen, but it is not necessary for your clients to be close to you. After all, isn't the point of working from home that all you need is a phone? (A computer and Internet are preferable but not necessary.) You can work for anyone in the country. (I had a lady in Missouri doing telemarketing for me for several years. We never met and I live in New Jersey. She simply kept track of her hours and leads and I mailed her a check. I even paid a portion of her phone bill.)

You are still thinking — give me more details on how to find the clients. Think about what are the areas of the country where people tend to make more money which means that the people and companies are used to paying more. As an example, you might live in Missouri or New Mexico where \$7 or \$8 an hour is a decent income, but the company or salesperson who you solicit to give you business is in New Jersey or New York or Boston where rates of pay are normally \$10 to \$12 an hour. This means you just earned more money for the same work just by soliciting business from areas which pay more than your area does.

Next, in the geographical target area of your choice, go online to Monster.com, Dice.com or Careerbuilder.com, etc. and look for those companies hiring salespeople. Call or write offering telemarketing services to make their sales professionals more productive by giving them a head start with qualified leads. This might just be a new concept for them so they might tell you that is what their salesperson is responsible for. Don't let that deter you. Just keep trying. Remember, every company must sell something in order to stay in business. The sales section is normally the thickest section of any "classified" section as every company's income is brought in through sales. Remember, there are thousands of companies looking for sales help in the entire country.

By using persistence anyone can persuade a company looking for sales assistance to give a persistent telemarketer a try. One technique is to say that they can try your services for free before committing. Think I am crazy? Think about it. If you are not making any money now, why not invest 5 hours of your time to prove to a company that it will pay off for them to hire you for a 20-30 hour a week commitment? If it does not work are you really any worse off than you were before? Another technique is for you to place a services available ad on Craigslist or other similar websites. Through companies such as VistaPrint you can even build your own website to advertise your services very inexpensively.

There is a section in this book which covers how to make effective telemarketing calls.

Other work from home service ideas are: child care, performing errands for a fee, typing services or research assistance for college students, personal assistant services for busy sales professionals and for small business owners.

Vivian Gaspar

As the Public Relations Director for an attorney specializing in mortgage modification, Vivian Gaspar has helped over 200 families to stay in their homes, and in some cases escape foreclosure all together. Ms. Gaspar had also been a recruiter, mortgage originator and a real estate agent. As a prior business owner she had been interviewed on television, newspaper and radio. Her business experience has helped her in advising her mortgage modification clients in their hardships.

Ms. Gaspar has been the founder and owner/operator of several businesses over the last 25 years. She has also been a public speaker on topics ranging from ID Theft to Mortgage Facts For Everyone. As someone who has worked individually with over 200 families in financial crisis in the last two years (as the Public Relations Director & Mortgage Modification Specialist in the legal office of V. James Castiglia in New Jersey) she heard similar stories and gave the same advice to people repeatedly. Her experience ranged from owning a marketing company to being a recruiter to being a mortgage loan officer which helped her in deciphering people's current mortgages as the first step in Mortgage Modification consultations. During the mortgage modification appointments she always started off by reviewing the client's origination documents to ensure that they had been fully aware of the specifics of their current mortgage. Unfortunately, Ms. Gaspar had found that over half of her modification clientele had been misled by the loan officer who placed those clients into the mortgage that currently needed modification.

Part of her responsibilities as Mr. Castiglia's Public Relations Director was to give speeches at civic organizations such as the Lions Clubs and Rotary Clubs. After several of these speeches, Ms. Gaspar had been approached with the suggestion to spread her knowledge to a wider audience and to consider writing a book. In February of 2010, she started giving the idea of writing a book on mortgage modification and the foreclosure process more serious consideration. Over the next few months Ms. Gaspar had concluded that she could help a wider base of people in crisis if she covered a broad subject base.

Ms. Gaspar started an outline of chapters on topics she wanted to see included in the book. Immediately she thought of all the business contacts she had accumulated over her years of attending business networking events, including those she organized and hosted. She was the founding member of the only lunch time Le Tip on the East Coast and founded her own location of Network Plus where the meetings were held every week for over a year. Ms. Gaspar had met several of the contributing authors at events which she hosted in 2009 and 2010 in Morris County, New Jersey. It was the knowledge of seasoned professionals that Ms. Gaspar wanted to bring to the general public. These topics had been created and outlined by Ms. Gaspar and included the expertise of 26 professionals in 38 chapters.

Ms. Gaspar's first book, "How to Survive Your Financial Crisis", is being released in February 2011 with the Spanish translation set to release in the Summer of 2012 along with a second edition as well as that edition's Spanish version to be released within 90 days thereafter.

Ms. Gaspar also envisioned the translation of both editions into the top 10 languages spoken throughout the world, with international sales and marketing through the website: www.howtosurviveyourfinancialcrisis.com.

SECTION 3

Valuable Information For All Business Owners & Sales Professionals

Introduction: You Are Not Your Business Card

by Ted Fattoross

You are not your business card. You are a person. Attending a networking function can be a little like dating. When you go out on a first date, would you propose marriage before even ordering your meal? Yet, for some reason that is exactly what we do — at both social and business networking events. We are not our business cards. Some people have the notion that once cards are exchanged this ritual is rite of passage to do or say anything. In truth, it's just a small piece of paper — smaller than a credit card and has a street value of about a nickel. It's who we are that really matters, not what we do. It's the size of our heart not our business card that's important. It's what we stand for, not what we sell that's relevant. It's who we associate with that defines us, not where we live or what we drive. It's why we do what we do that really counts. You are not your job — you are Infinite Opportunities, Unlimited Dreams and Ageless Beauty. We are not sharks in suits, we are eagles with wings.

Who am I? Just a guy, who at 4 AM woke up this morning and realized that most of us have been hypnotized at an early age and as adults have remained in this hypnotic state. For good reason we were taught not to talk to strangers. So we paid attention, became cautious, less curious. Locked our doors and closed our minds; put on the armor of the "right business suit". Went out and got business cards and communicate by phone and email — yes, even to the people sitting in the same room — both at home and at the office.

The wake up call? We are not children - we can talk to strangers. We can get to know the person at the check-out line, the bus, the train, the plane and bagel shop. We are not our business cards. We are people. People do not do business with business cards, they do business with people. So, maybe the real question is not what type style or color should I use on my business card. Maybe the real question is: "who am I"? And what do I stand for — and why do I do what I do? By the way, these questions are frightening - terrifying. But these are the real questions, the real deal. Are you the real deal? Too many people follow what I call the "family of origin script" and live a life not their own. Living the "family of origin script" is comfortable, safe and secure. In truth, it's a prison - three "hots and a cot" as they say behind bars. Safe. Leaving this place takes courage. Courage is not being fearless, courage is moving forward while facing our fear, period. Our real fear is not of failure. Our real fear is of possibility. Of what we are, of what we may become. Our real fear is that glimpse of amazing abundance, infinite wisdom, and boundless possibilities. We fear ourselves, our possibilities. Within each of us is a seed. A seed that must be planted, nurtured, cultivated and embraced. It's our seed — not mom's, dad's, our teachers, preachers or neighbor's. We own it and are responsible for its outcome. We own the outcome. We allow others to direct, dictate and manage us in an all-out effort not to take ownership of our lives - thus, avoiding the ownership of the outcome. We lose by default no matter how large our portfolio, value of our estate or size of our business. Never live by default. Own your seed, own your journey and celebrate the ownership of your outcome. Remind yourself that every day above ground is a great one - a gift, be thankful. Rejoice in all things. Please read the following poem I gave birth to when I first started my journey of sowing my seed. For the record, since then, I have not used a business card, completed over 6000 speaking events, over 100 consulting assignments and counseled over 1,000,000 people. I am not my business card, I am Infinite Opportunities, Unlimited Dreams and Boundless Energy who is inspired not only by the universe but by it's Master Artist - the Creator. Here is my poem - enjoy!

We are born complete,
we are not born deficient.
We need not be fixed,
for we are not broken.
We are whole, not fragmented.
We need to nurture the child in us,
not force it to grow up.
We are love, only love.
It is fear that prevents us from
being who we really are.
We are love, only love.

-Ted Fattorross-

PS - the greatest gift I am thankful for is the honor, the privilege and joy of being the daddy of Taylor and Jared Fattoross

Carpe Diem

Ted Fattoross
CEO/Founder
Joinnetworkplus.com
TedSpeak.com
Educational Services
Safe School Foundation
Ebony/Ivory

Ted Fattoross

Ted Fattoross, Network PLUS Founder and CEO, is a professional national speaker with 18 years experience leading people on the path of personal growth. He presents over 300 programs to over 250,000 people throughout America each year. From small school districts to corporate giants, from the classroom to the boardroom, Ted Fattoross has the knowledge and experience to lead programs on a wide variety of topics, as well as deliver the keynote address for your meeting, in-service and/or conference. He has been featured on national TV, radio programs, newspapers and provides over 300 programs each year for groups as small as 5 and as large as 5,000. Ted serves the corporate, government and non-profit markets in addition to the educational sector, on topics ranging from sales and customer service to teamwork and leadership. Teamwork, communicating effectively, relationship building, values and ethics are threaded through each program. Ted has been on the advisory board for Fortune 500 companies such as Tenneco and Union Camp.

His clients include American Express, Johnson & Johnson, Lucent, Bellemead, Cisco Systems, Ford, Merck, New York Stock Exchange, Lockheed, AT&T and American Management Association. Ted guarantees to exceed his clients expectations. A full line of corporate programs is available for any need. Ted has worked with companies large and small, helping motivate employees and teaching management new techniques, all of which are guaranteed to improve morale, and will increase sales!

His mission statement? "To inspire people to be the BEST they can be".

contact e-mail: tedfattoross@tedspeak.com

How To Get Your Business To Survive Tough Economies

by Neil Pinkman

What you need to do survive tough times are the same things you should be doing, not only in good economies but all the time. However, when times are tough business owners want the quick fix and shortcuts from what should be done all the time.

You need to develop a strategic plan not a business plan. Most small business owner, nine out of ten, do not have a strategic plan. Most people see having a small business as the equity for their retirement. Unfortunately, only two to ten percent of businesses are actually set up to be sold. One of the most critical elements is to have a business coach. All of the most successful businesses utilize business coaches and a strategic plan, re-visited frequently. A successful business is defined as one that operates profitably without the owner working in the business.

Also you need to develop a successful vision which goes out 10 – 15 years. Then the business owner needs to do an internal appraisal and external assessment that capture key assumptions – these combined with the vision equals the mission. The mission statement includes: how many people, how many locations, etc. Where do you want to be 24-36 months down the road in detail? From that you will derive critical goal categories. These should be 5-8 areas that must be addressed in order to meet the mission that drives to vision.

As an example of the 5 categories include: New product development; physical location; marketing; and staff and sales. They need to meet sufficiency and necessity tests.

Once you have 5-8 critical goal categories, then come up with specific goals for each category. Each category may have a dozen or more specific goals. Then each goal is broken to possible obstacles, then possible solutions, then specific action steps. These steps drive the budgets, the market plan and sales plan. Budget can also be broken down per category, this is normally done with a financial planner and CPA.

Regardless of where the business is, whether it is currently profitable or struggling and teetering on the edge of bankruptcy, it is critical to go through each of the above steps which forces you to see opportunities that are right in front of you all the time that you normally might not otherwise recognize.

The most common mistake being made in these very difficult economic times is that people are not re-investing in themselves and their business. They just put their head in the sand which will result in businesses being forced to fold / file bankruptcy.

MOST COMMON PATH TO FAILURE:

The biggest misconception in measuring the success of a business is that a successful business must have a lot of employees and be a large company. The real measure of a successful company is how much money the owner puts into his "pocket" at the end of each year AKA the most profitable with the least outlay for overhead.

Regardless of how bad times are: in every industry there is someone doing well and making a lot of money – this can be YOUR business if YOU have an effective strategic plan that you create and follow.

Examples of Companies that have re-invested in themselves:

1) Type of company: Construction – residential home remodeling

Time Frame starting with business coach: Oct / Nov 2008 to current

Age of company at start: 5 years old

At the start, this company's sales had plateaud, and the owner was concerned that sales would dangerously decline due to the economy and how others in the industry were performing. The owner hired a business coach and created and followed a strategic plan and identified new market segments which resulted in a growth rate of 30% per year in the last two years (during the recession of 2008-2010). During those 2 years many others in the same construction industry were forced to file bankruptcy or lay off many of their employees. These were deviating economic times for all the real estate and construction related industries.

2) Type of company: Graphic Design company (brochure and web design)

Time Frame starting with business coach: Sept/ Oct 2009

Age of company at start: 7 years

The reason for deciding to hire a business coach is that there was a sole owner who hired only freelance workers who desired growth. The primary step that was implemented was developing and following the strategic plan. The result of the strategic plan was that in 6 months the gross sales doubled and the owner hired a full time project manager.

3) Type of company: Holistic Wellness Center

Time Frame starting with business coach: 2002 - 2004

Age of company at start: 1 year

Unfortunately startup business's common mistake is that they get caught up in the excitement of the fun details of starting the business such as the business name, logo, marketing but fail to develop a strategy first and it is the strategy that defines who defines who those loyal customers are you are trying to attract and retain. Until you have done the strategy and know who your target market is you do not know who you are marketing to. This inevitably wastes much of the start up cash flow which is the reason for the famous ratio that 80% of business fail in the first 5 years.

When they first hired their business coach they had only 40 appointments per week. After 1 year they doubled the square footage of the business location, tripled their staff and grew to more than 120 appointments a week by simply creating, executing and closely following their strategic plan

Neil Pinkman

Neil Pinkman is a Regional Director for Paradigm Associates. Neil specializes in coaching entrepreneurs and small companies focused on brand development and growth.

Neil's passion is helping people become successful, both personally and professionally. Over the course of his three plus decades of experience as an entrepreneur, Neil has coached hundreds of people to achieve their goals. The wonderful result of Neil's extensive management, both of individuals and teams, is seeing how people and their organizations have thrived and prospered.

Neil's primary focus is helping individuals and organizations implement strategies to increase business, strengthen reputation, enhance personal development, and expand into new markets while utilizing their unique creative abilities. Neil's specialty areas include design companies, marine-related industries, and holistic practices.

Before becoming a Regional Director for Paradigm Associates, Neil established himself as a recognized trainer, coach, mentor, and business development manager. He began his career as founder and managing partner of an award-winning design and communication business consulting for both local and national accounts. Subsequently, he conceived of, created, and directed a holistic and wellness facility devoted to personal and spiritual well-being and health. This holistic approach center successfully served thousands of clients of all ages and from all walks of life, including those afflicted with cancer and allied diseases, eventually expanding not only to off-site trainings and sessions attended by the general public, but also producing successful spin-off businesses.

Neil's broad experience in all aspects of business development (advertising, marketing, sales training and trade shows) gives him great insight for helping others increase their ability to reach out for new business. Neil's easy-going, conversational style utilizing humor has allowed him to become a recognized speaker in the Union and Somerset County, NJ areas on the subjects of personal foundation, sales strategies, and family business development. He is involved in business organizations that serve the Bridgewater, Mountainside, New Providence, Summit, Warren, Watchung, and Westfield, NJ areas.

Neil Pinkman
Regional Director

Paradigm Associates
Breakthrough Thinking for Your Real World
1053 Sunny Slope Drive
Mountainside, NJ 07092
908-917-8203
npinkman@paradigmassociates.us
www.paradigmassociates.us

Your Business Plan - Yes, It Can Be A Daily Tool

by Jack Bleiberg, CPA

What is a Business Plan? Do small and medium sized businesses need to create business plans?

A business plan is a targeted communication of your vision. Moreover, a written business plan allows you the advantage of creating strategies that are well thought out and provides advanced notice of changes that may be needed at certain milestones. For a growing company, these changes can be for requirements such as financing, additions to staff and facilities, new layers of management, delegation of duties, etc. Even a company that is contracting must similarly consider when to release staff and find smaller space.

For the purpose of this chapter, I will refer to growing companies. But, please bear in mind that most companies have slow periods and even contracting companies need to prepare for these changes in order to survive.

An entity should always have multiple levels of plans. For example, one for the most likely future, one for a greater growth, and one for a lesser result. This allows management to have a guideline as to when and what actions must be taken, given the actual circumstances. If there is more than one decision maker, then changes according to the plan can be done without convening the group. If there is only one decision maker, that person can know that they can be gone for a period of time and their plans would be available to designated individuals (wouldn't it be nice to know that you can go on a longer vacation?). An important extension of this thought is that the plan can be used to communicate expectations and goals to your team.

There can be several "targets" of a business plan. The target is that person or group to whom the plan is being presented. Each target has its own unique concerns that must be addressed. So, in addition to the three planning levels described above, there should be iterations for specific users. The more common targets are:

• Internal - This is referred to as the "Strategic Plan." It is a deep consideration of where the corporate vision will go over time and how you plan to make it happen. This is the core business plan and will be our primary objective.

• Financing - Most lenders require a summary plan to support a loan application. In it, you must explain the use of proceeds and how it will be repaid. They must know that their risks are covered.

• Investors - To attract new capital, business plans are crucial. In many ways, the considerations are the same as the Financing plan, but also add the considerations of the return on investment and an exit plan for the investors.

• Talent Acquisition - Aspects of the plan may be used to attract new key staff members. They should not have access to all information, but they should be made excited by the vision and the part they will play.

• Spouse / Family – Never forget your spouse, family or significant other. You will be expending a lot of effort, passion and time on your company and possibly dedicating capital. You need to get them "aboard." By sharing your plans with them, they will feel a part of it, will understand what you are saying if you bring home success stories and frustrations, and they might even have a good idea that you have not yet considered. Again, too much information is not good. Unless that person is a partner or on your management team, consider sharing only the dream and the highlights. But, it is always better to include them in some way.

Basic questions to be answered:

- WHAT service or product does your business offer? What services or products are you considering to add / drop?

- WHY is there a demand for your product or service? Why would you be chosen over a competitor? What is unique and appealing about your product or service?

- WHO are the key people in your company? What is there business/professional history, education, industry background? Why are they special to this entity?

- WHERE is the demand? Is it geographic, demographic, etc.?

- WHEN will the plan be executed? What is the timeframe to start and complete? This may be as simple as a generic three year forecast, with no specific projects in mind.

What basic questions should be answered?

Most people think of a business plan as a mathematical / accounting exercise amounting to pages of spreadsheets. This is only a small part of it. Remember, the full plan is the communication of your vision. It needs to be largely narrative, graphics are great. The compulsory numbers are typically at the end and they serve to quantify your thoughts and to establish milestones (timeframe and amounts).

Minimally, the plan should include sections on:

- Marketing and Sales – how are you going to get knowledge of your products and services to your market. Then, how are you going to follow up and get the sale?

- Personnel – What skills do you need to execute the business plan? How available are these people and do you have any at your disposal? If not, how will you attract and retain good employees?

- Risk Management – This is a new hot button. Risk management includes identifying the risks of loss of physical and information assets and the safeguarding and insuring of those risks. See Chapter 15 by Terrance Coughlin of this book.

- Legal and Compliance – In our litigious society, how will the company minimize its risk from lawsuits by customers, staff and competitors, and how will we accomplish legal compliance, if appropriate.

- Financial – For internal plans, these analyses should be as detailed as possible. For external plans, they should be summarized and rounded. Double check the math! The schedules should include:
    - Use of proceeds, if this is for financing or investors.
    - Cash flow over the time period, usually by month.
    - Anticipated profit (loss) over the time period, usually by month (Return on Investment).
    - Exit plan – the repayment of debt or investment.

Methodology:

- Whatever you are comfortable in using is fine, so long as it is not a distraction to the process. It is critical that you think clearly and freely. Even if you write it manually and have it beautified later, make sure that your thoughts can flow unimpeded.

- Collaborative tools and techniques are the best approach. Try to never do a business plan on your own. We all tend to have "tunnel vision" and we need others to make sure that a realistic expression of your ideas is presented. If you are a sole proprietor, enlist a trusted friend, mentor or your accountant to be a sounding board for this.

• Software products have been specifically designed for creating business plans. But, they can be pricey. Basics, such as Microsoft's Excel and Word, are popular and are sufficient. There are templates available on the internet.

• Consider that the plan must be easy to update over time. No one can see the future precisely, and you will need to update your plan frequently.

• Remember, methodology is the only tool. Do not obsess on it.

<u>Three Do's and Three Don'ts:</u>

DO: Make the effort to create at least the strategic plan.

DO: Make periodic updates to it so that if the business does better or worse, you will be prepared.

DO: Enlist all of your partners and / or management to participate. If you have none, find a mentor.

DON'T: Go through all of this effort and never look at it again! Plan to compare actual results to the plan at least quarterly. Use this analysis to understand variances and adjust the future plan.

DON'T: Be discouraged if reality is different that the plan. Take corrective action quickly. A benefit of this work is that you will be able to recognize aberrations quickly and adjust accordingly. No Surprises!

DON'T: Keep this secret. It is important to communicate your vision to the other involved players, such as management, your accountant and attorney, key consultants (as appropriate) and your spouse.

Jack Bleiberg, CPA

Jack is a practicing CPA who has a developed proficiency in guiding companies to reach their full potential through proper planning and execution, and maximizing operational efficiencies and controls. He also works with his clients to protect their wealth with proper tax, business exit and estate planning. Jack has worked with all sizes of entities, from small through large public companies.

Jack has been a partner at a regional CPA firm, and owned and operated business systems and consulting firms. Jack has over twenty-five years of experience owning and operating small businesses. He has extensive experience across many industries.

Jack is a graduate of Lehigh University, where he obtained a Bachelors degree in Accounting He has been published in the CPA Journal and chaired a committee of the NJ Society of CPAs. Jack is currently Vice President and Executive Board Member at the Daughters of Israel Geriatric Center in West Orange, NJ. He is a member of the American Institute of CPAs, the NJ Society of CPAs, and is active with the North Essex Chamber of Commerce.

Contact Information: Jack@JBleibergCPA.com
Website: www.JBleibergCPA.com

In Person Business Networking

by Philip Doyle

Those who attend networking events are in the business of building long-lasting relationships that will hopefully lead to increased business for the ambitious sales executive or small business owner. As a sales professional, former small-business owner, and long-time "guerilla" networker, I often observe networking event attendees that behave like robotic automatons when interacting with would-be prospects. All too often, these individuals focus solely on their canned speech, and not on engaging with the prospect at a deeper level. The result of course is a prospect that assumes a defensive posture. I realized early on that sales people and business owners need to focus on opening doors for their clients and prospects in order to increase their own business; or as Zig Ziglar once quipped, "You can have everything you want in life if you help enough people get what they want".

You will close more business by building a network of relationships and by endorsing others by giving sales leads and by endorsing those within your network. When you bring leads to your referral network, it will be returned to you tenfold, not just in the leads and endorsements referred your way by your network, but also in the new relationships formed as a result of the new leads and endorsements. It is the gift that keeps on giving and is returned to you in multiples.

One of the simplest ways to expand your horizons is to partner with companies that offer products and services that compliment your own product or service offerings. Also, seek out industries that target the same or similar markets that you do, so that you may form partnerships in this space as well. An example of this would be a mortgage loan officer partnering with a credit repair person.

Another good pearl of wisdom is that when attending networking events, do not just be a business card collector. This is not a contest. You are there to connect – to identify a handful of prospects who you want to forge relationships with. Strike up a good conversation with worthy candidates. It is also very important to attend events where everyone has an opportunity to introduce themselves so that you can listen carefully to see who is a good fit to co-market with. Also, if someone else's clients and supplies are good possible connections for you; even better someone YOU can help. Then they will feel the desire to reciprocate by introducing you to their client base or suppliers.

The best way to get the most benefit for the long term by creating networking connections is to belong to one or two organizations and form close relationships with members instead of going to miscellaneous events and collecting cards and hoping to land the instant client by chance. You need to evaluate your own networking on a person by person basis by evaluating individual situations. Bring your database to the relationship so that it is reciprocated on an individual basis to multiply your efforts. You need to make the effort on an individual basis, per relationship, to balance the scales of referrals.

One excellent way to find new networking meetings is www.meetup.com. The author of this chapter is the president and founder of 24/7Networking Sales which hosts several networking meetings each month.

Philip Doyle

Mr. Doyle is a graduate of Accounting from Fairleigh Dickinson University.

It is Mr. Doyle's proud honor to hold an Honorable Discharge from the United States Marine Corps.

Mr. Doyle has worked for several companies developing a well rounded background in production, logistics, finance, purchasing, customer service and sales. After having worked in just about all areas of a company, he was able to help companies solve problems from being able to see each areas perspective on the problem.

This has helped him in coming up with solutions for his clients, being able to see how different companies can work together to develop more sales by cross selling and up selling.

Philip Doyle has been responsible for sales activities in customer service, sales budgeting, customer relationships, producing and delivering product to customers, solving customer/product problems including logistics since 1994.

Mr. Doyle is the president and founder of 24-7 Networking Sales, a company he started in 2002, which generates sales leads for companies. Around 2004, an idea came to him to start a unique networking group and which shares commissions. Overnight the idea blossomed into a company which became a networking and sales organization. The company continues to enjoy tremendous success helping clients pick up new business and foster new relationships both small business owners and sales professionals alike.

Currently 24/7 Network Sales is expanding into Manhattan in 2011 after experiencing rapid growth in New Jersey.

Philip J. Doyle
24-7 Networking Sales, LLC
President
58 Valley Tr.
Oak Ridge, NJ 07438
973-697-8872
973-858-0302 FAX
PDoyle@24-7NetSales.com
www.24-7NetSales.com
Proud Member of the Marine Corps League

Health and Life Insurance For The Business Owner

by Harry Herbst

Being a small business owner today, especially in this economy, is no easy proposition. Salaries aside, employee benefits are the single largest expense for any business owner. In an economy where small business profits can be down (in many cases) by fifty-percent, the cost of benefits on average still increase in the neighborhood of twenty-five percent each year. This, along with increased expenses across the board in other areas, is enough to give any small business owner significant anxiety. Of course, in this day and age employees are being asked to contribute a larger percentage into the employee benefit pool, and if the math doesn't work out for the small business owner, then hours get reduced and employees start to lose their jobs.

When we speak of benefits, we are speaking for the most part about health insurance, so we will focus our discussion on this. A decade ago most business owners had a one-hundred percent plan that included out-of-network benefits. Year after year these benefits are significantly "watered down". Fast forward to today and it is not difficult to see that the benefits that employees receive are but a fraction of what they were in another time and place.

First:

A separate deductible for those who have been hospitalized, known as a hospital co-pay rider.

Second:

A split co-payment in the form of a higher co-payment for specialists versus your primary care physician. For example, a visit to your primary care physician may cost $20, whereas a trip to the specialist is $50. A primary care physician today is inclusive of an internist, obstetrician, or pediatrician. All others are more or less considered to be specialists.

The elimination of out-of-network coverage is basically known as a Health Maintenance Organization (HMO). What this means is that in order to be covered, you must use all in-network services. If the physician does not participate in your plan, then you do not have reimbursable benefits. Most small businesses utilize an HMO type of plan.

A one-hundred percent plan is indicative of no out-of-pocket expenses. Today's plans more closely resemble eighty, seventy, or even fifty percent plans that are indicative of having to satisfy a deductible before coverage begins.

Out of pocket expenses. Prescription drug benefits – As medications become more expensive, this requires the participant to have greater out of pocket expenses. Rx benefits are one of the major contributors to increases in insurance premiums. The elimination of some basic services such as MRI's, cat scans and other services become out of pocket expenses in an effort to reduce premiums.

Concurrently, premiums continue to sky rocket.

Ancillary benefits such as dental and vision benefits have become luxury benefits and unaffordable to many small business owners, whereas a decade ago it was considered mainstream for these benefits to be covered.

There has been much conversations from the current administration to address these issues. In fact, health reform has been on the forefront and has been a priority for president Obama. Unfortunately there has been much confusion and frustration in this regard. At this point in time the small business owner has not witnessed any relief.

These contributing factors do not present for a very positive forecast for the small business owner in New Jersey as well as many other states. The stress and anxiety levels are increasing rapidly causing a ripple effect which will inevitably cause hardship for not just the small business owners and their employees but, on a large scale, the economy as a whole. Furthermore, in many instances the end result will be that many small business owners will be forced to "fold their tents" and shut their doors, causing additional unemployment.

Harry Herbst

Mr. Herbst is a licensed insurance agent who started in 1975. He started his own Insurance Agency in 2002 working with small business owners in small employee benefits arena. Mr. Herbst is a member of the National Association of Insurance agents and Financial Advisors NAIFA. He is also a member of the National Association of Health Underwriter NAHU and was awarded a membership to the prestigious Million Dollar Round Table (MDRT.)

Mr. Herbst also proudly served his country as a US Navy Veteran. He is also Senior Vice Commander of the Jewish War Veterans and a Trustee of Freehold Jewish Center. Active in the various Networking Associations and Chambers of Commerce.

Mr. Herbst holds a BA from the City University of New York and has an MA from the New School for Social Research.

HARRY HERBST & ASSOCIATES
Insurance & Financial Planning
708 Ginesi Drive
Suite 206
Morganville, NJ 07751
(732) 536-5200
(732) 536-5201 (Fax)
1-888-786-5201 (toll free)

Cold Calling Tips For Business Owners And Salespeople

by Deborah Anderson

Cold Calling Tips for Everyone – Business Owners & Sales People alike

Many small businesses live and die by the strength of their internal sales force. Dialing for dollars as it is affectionately referred to, is the bread and butter for many businesses. Each telemarketer brings their own brand of sales experience and personality to the table, and it is the goal of every small business owner with a telemarketing sales force to find the magic formula to replicate the very best of their thundering herd. Below are some useful tips and information in your attempts to replicate the very best that you have.

The most successful tips:

Be a good listener, respond accordingly. Adjust your tone to mirror the other person's.

Do not take negative reaction personally. You don't know if you just caught that person running to the phone after spilling their coffee and were just annoyed at that, and not necessarily anything that you had to say.

Approach every dial as a brand new opportunity! Do not let the last call's negativity affect the next call.

Having a positive attitude really does shine through in the tone of your voice. Keeping a smile on your face, even though they cannot see it, will also shine through.

Attitude is EVERYTHING. When someone is only "meeting" you over the phone their senses are heightened just like a blind person's other senses are more acute. How you come across over the phone is their entire impression of you.

How you introduce yourself leaves an everlasting impression throughout the entire conversation, and it creates the tone leading up to your call's objective. It also directs the conversation and is a guideline which will lead you to your ultimate goal for that call.

Speak slowly and deliberately. Think more carefully than if you were in person.

Watch your Um's and Ah's, try to sound relaxed.

Always be courteous, regardless of the prospect or clients reaction. Never hang up on anyone.

Be sure to provide a phone number where they can call you back. It is a Federal Law.

Take notes. This way, when someone says to call them back, you have a more familiar tone with which to start off the return call. As an example — Fred says call me after I get back from my vacation in Hawaii so when you do call back you can ask how was his trip and more details to relax him which will lower his guard, such as which islands did he visit?

Get a headset or Bluetooth so you never "put the receiver down."

Expect to make 20 – 30 calls per hour.

Never leave a message. Hang up after 3 rings.

Think of selling as helping to solve someone's problem. In telemarketing you are always trying to find the people who have that problem.

The DO NOT CALL list: When they ask you to put them on the list — make sure that you do not call them back! The fine can be as high as *$11,000 per offense* if they choose to press charges.

- If the prospect asks to be put on the "do not call list" — Say "I am sorry to have bothered you", and make a "list".

- For consumer lists — ensure you buy a "scrubbed list". This is the responsibility of the list company you buy your list from. Ask for details that the list was scrubbed quarterly.

- Top Recommended list company: Info USA.

IN SUMMARY - Sales is a numbers game. View every rejection as one less you need to experience before your next call or sale. Expect objections and have your rebuttals ready. Listen and try to learn from each rejection and use it as an opportunity to improve.

Deborah Anderson

Ms. Anderson holds a BA from Rutgers University and a Masters Degree from Fordham University. Her extensive background in marketing and sales started in high school working for various newspapers and contractors.

Upon completion of her master's degree in 1989, it was the height of the recession and the most beneficial opportunities presented themselves in marketing and sales.

After a short career in the financial industry in banking, Ms. Anderson found success in working days for a market research firm and evenings as a manager for a telemarketing company. Ms. Anderson has seen how rewarding life owning a telemarketing/sales company now in her 18th year working with sales executives and corporations ranging from AT&T to Prudential.

Ms. Anderson's other areas of expertise include telemarketing and sales training for fortune 500 companies as well as single executives. These industries range from financial advisors, mortgage brokers, etc. Also, Ms. Anderson has been published in a variety of Who's Who publications for successful executives and interviewed a few times on Channel 12 news

Future Waves Marketing
South Brunswick, New Jersey
Ph: 732-274-9399
futwavmkt@aol.com

Low /No Cost Benefits to Retain Employees

by Katherine Woodfield Hermes

Thinking outside the box and opening your mind to employee life management issues is about more than just health insurance. Voluntary benefits, while not on a par with health coverage or retirement programs, are increasingly being added to employers' menus of employee benefits. Employers facilitate the availability of the benefits and employees individually choose and pay for those benefits that meet their needs in their lives. As long as employees are being asked to foot a portion of the bill, they should have some say in what they are paying for, right?

Voluntary benefits, also called worksite benefits, have been around for decades. They range from niche products such as pet insurance and identity-theft protection to coverage categories with wider appeal, such as automobile and homeowners insurance. Employees' costs are often based on discounted group rates negotiated by the employer. The employer's expenses are typically limited to administrative costs, such as those for payroll deduction.

Some voluntary benefits are portable — meaning the employee can continue the coverage after leaving the company. Although some insurance benefits are sold as group policies, most are individual policies. The most popular benefits are still basic benefits — voluntary life and voluntary disability, however there is a fast growing category of benefits that consists of specialized medical coverage. Some types of coverage in that category are being expanded. For example, critical-illness insurance that once covered only cancer has been broadened in many instances to include heart attacks, major organ transplants, and other specific medical conditions or procedures. Typically, a lump-sum benefit of $10,000 to $50,000 is paid after a covered event occurs, and the money can be spent on medical or nonmedical needs.

When choosing a voluntary-benefits provider, consultants suggest, look for vendors that have experience with voluntary benefits, that have top financial ratings from A.M. Best or similar insurance rating agencies, and that offer excellent customer service and administration. Like most things in life, you get what you pay for and the cheapest product isn't necessarily the best.

The secret to success is implementation and that means collaborating with vendors. The HR role is to quarterback the whole process, meaning the HR person needs to have a handle on what's being done and who's doing it. Generally, HR sets up payroll deductions, facilitates communication with employees, monitors providers and integrates providers' information with the employer's intranet. Included in this category are such items as life insurance, long-term care insurance, disability insurance, prepaid legal services, pet health insurance, and identity-theft protection. If an employee purchases automobile or homeowners' insurance through payroll deductions, rather than installments, the costs are automatically budgeted. Through some plans, employees can save $400 to $500 a year.

Some employers also subsidize voluntary benefits to sweeten the deal for participants. The gesture of generosity doesn't usually cost much as any benefit might have 30 – 40% employee participation and the costs are usually small as compared to the figures to which one is accustomed with respect to health care premiums.

The real question is, why not? Voluntary insurance plans can resolve a bevy of market pressures faced by HR and benefits managers today, at no cost to their companies. As a unique opportunity to satisfy competing priorities, voluntary insurance programs accomplish the seemingly impossible—help create robust, affordable benefits packages in the face of diminishing budgets, rising healthcare costs, and a heated competition for talent.

Growing financial stress among employees can decrease morale, satisfaction and productivity. Nearly one quarter of employers believe they are more likely to lose employees to competitors with better benefits packages.[1]

Employees feel that no other workplace benefit comes close in terms of importance.[2] Among employers who currently or previously provided voluntary insurance, the top reasons are to:

- Retain employees (23%).
- Increase job satisfaction (20%).

A company's benefits offerings affects its abilities to recruit and retain top talent.

Thinking Outside the Box About Health Insurance

The cost of health care continues to outpace inflation and household earnings at a pace greater than 2 to 11%. To reduce the burden on corporate bottom lines, benefits decision-makers are often forced to pass larger portions of these increases onto their workforce. The result, however, is that employees are now faced with some tough decisions, with many resorting to drawing from personal savings, dipping into retirement accounts, and increasing use of credit–all of which can lead to personal bankruptcy. When an employee faces financial difficulties, an employer feels the impact as well in the form of decreased job performance, absenteeism and dissatisfaction. At the same time, HR managers remain tasked with attracting and retaining the best employees.

1 (Small Business "Now More Than Ever" Aflac, Acceler-PULSE™, 2009),

2 (Market Structure: Decision-Makers," TNS Taylor Nelson Sofres, 2006.)

For reasons I find very hard to fathom, many American's have a difficult time taking responsibility for their own health care. We pay for things all day long, but we don't want to pay to go to see the doctor.

We cut health care costs and improve our personal health care when we understand how health insurance is structured, and change to the highly beneficial Consumer Directed Health Care (CDHC).

Reorienting consumers is a difficult and uphill battle which cuts broker's commissions in half. Brokers can neither afford the time to explain this concept nor the loss of income that results from offering health insurance policies for half of the current rates.

Most health insurance consists of a "maintenance contract" and "catastrophe contract." Eliminate the maintenance contract and most Americans get healthier and save money.

Analogy: Home and auto owners pay for maintenance and insure against disaster. Following that successful structure, everyone who has a body should be responsible for general upkeep while being protected from disaster.

VP Insurance is designed to indemnify (protect) you and your assets. Out of control costs stem from looking to disaster indemnification providers to pay for our common low-risk or no-risk expenses.

In our current HMO/PPO/POS system, we pay for both 'maintenance plan' and 'catastrophe policy.' The disaster part of the policy covers the lion's share of risk for the individual, and yet, significant consumer cost goes towards the maintenance aspect of our policies.

Most people pay more in maintenance premiums then they claim in benefits - 80% of American's pay less than $700 per year in medical expenses. Why pay an additional $1500 premium PLUS a co-pay, so that the insurance will pay maintenance costs of $700 MINUS the co-pay?

Our current health insurance model is a two part plan with a single premium that seamlessly, expensively and unnecessarily provides both maintenance and disaster coverage. Most people do not realize that they can split apart those two components, save money, and better protect themselves and their families.

The solution is a High Deductible Health Plan (HDHP) or a Consumer Directed Health Plan (CDHP) linked to a Health Savings Account (HSA). Money we save in premiums (cash spent which we never see again) is instead invested into an HSA where cash accumulates tax deductible and tax free to pay future medical costs for ourselves and our families- the money is ours to keep.

Patients are empowered- costs drop as we comparison shop and negotiate routine bills. Doctors benefit as they are free to attend patient health instead of insurance forms, multiple invoices, and collections. Insurance companies gladly pay for annual check-ups and preventative care, without deductible or co-pay to incentivize people to stay healthy. The escalating cost of billing and claims processing dramatically decrease as we eliminate multiple layers of unnecessary middle men.

Most important (and astonishing), returning to our analogy- just as people maintain their own cars and homes far better than the rentals they live in and drive, McKinsey & Co. statistics prove that with personal financial benefit, 25% of people make healthier choices.

The first step towards improving the current health insurance system is education- reorienting every American towards taking responsibility for their body maintenance, and towards health insurance as the indemnity plan for which it is designed. This becomes easy as we see the cash we are not wasting in premiums quickly accumulating in our own HSA bank accounts.

Other Benefits Your Employees Will Love

Employees of the sandwich generation have to balance the responsibility of their jobs, their families and caring for a sick or elderly loved one. Hence, they are sandwiched between and often responsible for family members of both the previous and next generation. An estimated $33 billion is lost due to turn over, replacement, stress, lost productivity and care giving related absences. However, employers can work with Patient Advocates to alleviate some of this stress and to improve productivity, for example My Health Care Connect , www.myhealthcareconnect.com. Employees who retain the services of Patient Advocates report better personal health and less stress than those who had no access to support. Employers who recognize these issues earn their employees loyalty.

If you own a home, at some point it will need some attention. Broken furnaces, no heat, no water, home repairs of all shapes and sizes take employee's minds off of their jobs. Being a resource for trusted contractors will be a tremendous relief for an employer. Every business is tough and Home Remodeling is no exception. The ability to recommend a contractor and leverage your firms continued support, is a valuable and free offering. We found BBJ Inc. Remodelers www.bbjremodelers.com in New Jersey. They strive for total customer satisfaction, have an amazing reputation and are an awesome resource for your employees.

Another no cost great benefit employers can offer their employees is help finding a used car. Car problems cause unexpected and unwelcome delays in work and productivity. A service that helps car buyers locate, test and negotiate for high quality pre-owned cars that fit their budget can save both the employer and the employee from a potentially explosive situation. Auto Hunters, such as www.findpreownedcars.com can save time, stress and money. With a net work of 300 dealers nationwide they can stress test the pre-owned vehicles and notify the buyer when a good deal has arrived that fits the request.

Katherine Woodfield Hermes

Ms. Woodfield Hermes has almost two decades of experience working for pharmaceutical giants. She had been exposed to almost every type of health care insurance sold in America. Ms. Woodfield Hermes had worked with doctors and office managers to help them get paid for their reimbursements, and had a unique view on how the patients' families struggled under the weight of unexpected expenses.

As an independent broker, she is able to evaluate each company for the best medical plan available and additionally offer employees the option to choose benefits on a voluntary basis at no cost to the employer. Ms. Woodfield Hermes able to use my knowledge of how the doctors are paid, the insurance companies pay, and help employees avoid financial hardship.

Katherine Woodfield Hermes
kwhermes@verizon.net
contact phone: 908-421-5381

Your Local Printer Is Better Than Vista Print? Yes!

by Gerry Harris

The day has come – The annual networking event that you've been waiting for all year. Sure, you're a member of your local networking chapter of twenty regulars on a weekly basis, but that's like Cheers, everyone there knows you. This event is different; there will be well over a thousand people, all potential prospects and potential clients just waiting for you to dazzle them with your personality and wares. You don your best suit, freshly pressed, of course. You put on the shoes you polished the night before. Then it happens - As you walk through the golden arches to meet your first potential prospect, hand extended, you pull out a business card… from Vista Print. Vista Print allows individuals to obtain business cards extremely cheaply or at no charge. Of course, there's no free lunch in life. The catch is that Vista Print's logo appears on the back of your business card, sort of like time-sharing.

Well, you almost had it. The sale, that is. But then "almost" only counts in horseshoes and hand grenades. Consider this: Your competition invests a lot of money to convince your would-be clientele that they can produce and deliver a better product or service than you can. Your vendors invest a lot of money to convince you that they are the best resource to deliver the product or service to suit your need. It is a fair bet that your competition or vendors did not opt to print out business cards "free of charge" at Vista Print or the like. Chances are that at the very least they made a modest investment in business stationary that does not look cheap or promote another company. Making this sort of first impression gives the recipient the feeling that they're not worth good stationary.

There's a difference between frugal and cheap. Knowing this difference will help you to keep your own costs down, while adding value where needed. Knowing how to see the forest through the trees will help you considerably. In short, your prospects will interpret your frugality negatively.

As far as first impressions go, one factoid that we can all bank on in life is that perception is reality, where the wrong impression can open up a Pandora's Box of opportunities to pass judgment on the person standing in front of you for the first time. Or worse, it could be you that is the object of negative judgment.

As an entrepreneur, although you may have marketing material and a website to promote your business, handing someone a business card from Vista Print or the like sends the message that you either have no money (i.e., not successful), or that the recipient not worth the investment in a quality stationary – the most basic of fundamentals. There's nothing wrong with Vista Print or similar company, per se. Just don't expect to be taken seriously by your prospects or your customers (unless you're representing Vista Print).

At the end of the day, the goal is to meet or exceed your prospects expectations. Develop a relationship with a reputable local printer like us at B&L Printing who will be your business partner for all your marketing needs.

Gerry Harris

Gerry Harris, president of B&L Printing Co. Inc. in Hillsborough, NJ, has extensive experience in both retail/wholesale sales and the printing industry.

A firm believer in giving back to the community, Gerry is a member of Rotary International District 7510, District Chair for Interact, and a Boy Scout leader on a regional level. He is still active as an assistant scoutmaster, District Eagle Board of Review, and District Committee member. In 2005, Gerry was the 94th person in the world to receive the Cliff Docherman Award of Achievement.

This book was produced by B&L Printing, which has been in existence for over twenty-five years.

Feel free to contact Gerry for any of your questions on how professional printers can make a tremendous impact on your business's bottom line.

B&L Printing Co. Inc.
46 Old Camplain Road
Hillsborough, NJ 08844
Tel 908-707-1311
Fax 908-707-4067
sales@blprinting.com

Insurances Every Business Owner Must Have

by Terrance Coughlin CPCU, ARM, AIC

Any size business must have the following insurance: Anyone who is a direct sales representative or has formed any type of a corporate entity.

~ **Property insurance (including renters)**

1) Consists of real property and business owned content – make sure whatever you own you have adequate insurance coverage. Examine leases – your landlord might require either fire legal or tenant legal liability insurance which are to protect his real property in case your negligence caused the damage.

~**Commercial liability-** There to protect the business in the event if someone is harmed, regardless of where the person is harmed, by the business entity or employees. Liability insurance is broken down into several parts.

First is the per occurrence which is the most coverage the policy will afford for any one occurrence.

Second is the general aggregate or total amount of insurance which will be afforded under the policy, many policies can give per occurrence i.e. 1 million per occurrence and 2 million for the total aggregate of the policy. This can possibly be insufficient for possible lawsuits. This is where umbrella/ excess policy is useful.

Third, products and completed operations – if your product or service is a likely source of claims many carriers will use this to limit your claim. Example, a hammer where the shaft breaks and the hammer breaks and hurts someone you can be sued for making a faulty shaft. You will more than likely have multiple claims. This policy type is where the product when completed is now in the hands of a 3rd party. This policy is used if once completed product is shown to have had a design flaw had contributed to someone's being injured.

Fourth, Professional Services / "Errors & Omissions" aka "E&O"– many policies can exclude professional services, i.e. Attorneys, engineers, accountants even hairdressers. The cause of damage is derived from the fault of the application of the specialized area of knowledge. There can be industry specific terms for this type of insurance. This policy is normally purchased separately.

Cost saving tip: some carriers will afford an "all in one" policy for very small businesses and you can get a discount for buying from one source.

~ **Commercial Auto** – even if you do not have a corporately owned vehicle you still need auto insurance, – many people assume a companies auto insurance only applies to the vehicles the company owns. This is completely wrong. One of the more likely sources of litigation company might have is the liability if you are in a car on company business and have a car accident. The business entity can be sued regardless of who owns the vehicle. Personal Insurance may protect the driver but will not extend to the corporate entity. Business would need to procure "Non owned and hired auto liability." This is to protect the entity when an employees is driving a personal vehicle for business purposes. This can be purchased one of two ways, if the entity owns vehicles it can be included on the corporate auto policy or attached to general liability coverage section. If any company entity owns the vehicle then they need to insure it under business's name and ensure that the auto coverage suits the possible exposure. This can be the number one source of exposure since it is more likely and this is extremely low cost.

~ **Workman's Compensation** - Policy meant to protect the worker not the business. All work comps are set by the state in which the individual is working. Even if you have no employees many states still require you to purchase workman's compensation. This can cover anyone you have contracted to work with you. You can be covered as a business owner and you can opt in.

~**Umbrella / Excess Policies** - in many events many of the limits afforded by the general liability, (all categories listed above) are not high enough to properly protect the entity. It can be more affordable and cost effective to buy this additional policy can be sold separately or in conjunction with other types of policies. This will depend on how you are buying it and from whom.

Remember these are the minimum coverage in the broadest of terms for the details which best suited for your and your business. Please contact a local insurance professional for further information.

Terrence Coughlin,

CPCU, ARM, AIC

Terrence P. Coughlin, CPCU, ARM, AIC is a professional Insurance and Risk Management Consultant with nearly thirty years of finance and insurance experience. He is the principle of Task Risk Management Consulting, Inc, located in Wyckoff, NJ. He has held senior positions in the finance and insurance brokerage arenas before spending the last ten years as a Risk Management Consultant.

In addition to his hands-on experience, Terrence has also worked hard on the technical/academic side; earning the Charter Property and Casualty Underwriter (CPCU) designation, which is the most advanced designation in the insurance industry. In addition to earning his CPCU, he has also earned his Associate in Risk Management (ARM) and Associate in Claims (AIC) Designations.

Terry Coughlin continues to keep up-to-date on his insurance knowledge by teaching CPCU and ARM courses on a regular basis. He is also a member of the Society of Risk Management Consultants (SRMC) and is a Past President of the New Jersey Chapter of the CPCU Society.

Task Risk Management Consulting, Inc.
Terrence P. Coughlin, President
CPCU, ARM, AIC
245 Braen Ave, Suite F
Wyckoff, NJ 07417
(201) 425.8363 Office
(201) 425.8398 Fax
coughlin@taskrmc.com email
taskrmc.com website

Practical Marketing For Every Business's Budget

by Ronald Hatcher

What line item is usually among the first to be cut from the budget when business is slow? You probably surmised that it is advertising and other forms of marketing a company's products or services. There are times when this is an absolute necessity, but keep this in mind: Marketing and advertising are the lifeblood of any business. Study upon study has shown that businesses that cut back marketing budgets, significantly, suffer greater business slumps than those businesses that reduce spending slightly or don't cut the budget at all.

If working with a small budget is unavoidable, it doesn't mean that you should throw up your hands, say, "I give up", and just put the money in your pocket? Absolutely not! Advertising is not really an expense. It is an investment. You do not stop investing, simply because you have less money to invest. If you are a smart investor, you seek out investment advice, and you also seek low-cost investments that still offer a good rate of return. Apply this same principle to advertising and you can reap big rewards from small expenditures.

Here's a list of things you can do to market your business without breaking the bank. *It is not all-inclusive, but illustrates the diversity of approaches. Some of these, you can do yourself, while others should be handled by a marketing professional. Enlisting the help of a professional is often less expensive than you think. In fact, if you are buying media such as TV, Radio, Print, Outdoor or certain forms of Online, the media professional is paid a commission by the media, thereby making the professional's services to you free.*

1. Television – You don't have to buy a spot on The Super Bowl for $3 million to make a splash. Local Cable TV is more affordable than many business owners think. You can keep your costs down by buying only one cable system within your business' core geography. Most important of all, producing the commercial can cost as little as $2,000. Better yet, it may be produced for **free** by the cable system that your TV commercial will run on. In other words, if you purchase a schedule from the cable operator, they may produce your commercial for free.

Another means of reducing costs is to purchase a "DR" schedule. DR (direct response) rates are lower, however the cable operator reserves the right to not run any spots that comprise your DR schedule if they can be sold for higher, "regular advertiser" rates. The nuances of planning and negotiating a TV schedule are such that you may want to enlist a professional's assistance because they can usually save you money and save you a few headaches along the way.

2. Radio – Here's a little secret: You do not need to buy a lot of radio spots for a successful campaign. On more than one occasion, I have seen a single radio commercial generate telephone calls and website visits. By the way, these were not award-winning commercials. They were simple and to the point, but they struck a chord with the listeners and left them with a way to get in touch with the business. The last point is the most important point. Make sure the commercial says the phone number and/or web address a **minimum** of two times. If possible, three times is better.

If you can't afford to hire a copywriter to do a script for you, it is okay. Write the first draft yourself. You can submit this to the radio station(s) and they will usually edit it and record it for free.

Radio advertising costs vary greatly depending on the size of the market, the size of the audience listening to the station, the time of year and the time of day that the commercial will run and the actual supply of available commercial time that the station has to sell. A spot in a market such as New York or Los Angeles will cost much more than a spot in Pueblo or Texarkana *(TV costs vary for the same reasons)*.

Radio schedules costing as little as $1,000 have proven to be effective in big markets such as New York. So, depending upon where your business is based, you can scale it down accordingly.

3. Print – The Internet has hurt Print more than any other media category. This spells opportunity for savvy entrepreneurs. Publishers are more accommodating than ever before. The costs for advertising in newspapers and magazines are highly negotiable. The most important thing to keep in mind is that larger size ads will usually garner more readership, but generally speaking, the law of diminishing returns is in effect. What this means, for instance, is that a full-page ad will usually not deliver double the sales of a half page ad nor will a half page deliver twice as many sales as a quarter page. Most studies suggest that there is better return-on-investment (ROI) in smaller ad sizes relative to larger sizes.

In order to keep your costs down, design an attractive ad, but one that limits itself to the most vital information and can be relatively small. It's better to run two small ads than one large one. Message frequency will help your customers remember you. You will also reach a slightly larger audience because not everyone reads every issue of a publication.

There are some publications that will actually run advertising on a pay-per-lead basis. The marketer only pays the publisher for legitimate leads. This is not a common practice, but it's worth exploring, since it can result in tremendous savings.

Community newspapers and other weekly and bi-weekly publications, such as The PennySaver also deliver great results for many marketers without requiring huge outlays. If you see one of your competitors running in the PennySaver virtually every week, that's a sure sign that it is worth testing. A half page, full color ad with a circulation of 50,000 can be purchased for around $500. Again, negotiation is the order of the day. If you don't have the time to haggle, get a professional to do it for you. You will save money and recapture the time you need to run your business.

Ads in school yearbooks are very inexpensive and subject to repeat exposure over several years.

4. Direct Mail – As many of you know, doing a direct mail campaign for your individual company can be expensive. Interestingly, though, it remains a staple for so many small businesses because it still works and in many cases delivers one of the best ROI's available. There are ways to keep your costs down and still get the benefits that direct mail offer. If your product or service lends itself to be among other marketer's offerings, consider one of the cooperative or group mailing products available, such as ValPak. ValPak's famous blue envelope has come to represent savings for most Americans. If you want to "jump-start" your sales consider a coupon or some type of promotion that will drive response. You can reach about 50,000 homes for $1,000 to $2,000.

Welcome Wagon is a direct marketing program that targets new homeowners. About 16% of Americans move each year. Of the 16%, nearly half move to a different county. Welcome Wagon offers a few low-cost solutions to target the newest arrivals in your neighborhood.

5. Out-of-home / Outdoor – Anyone who has ever investigated the cost of a billboard (or bulletin as the largest units are referred to) knows that they can be very expensive. Some spectacular units in markets such as New York, Chicago and Los Angeles can cost upwards of $100,000 per month. However, this media category has seen tremendous growth, second only to that of the Internet. The increase in available options offers an opportunity for the astute marketer. Take a walk around your core business zone. Look for signage and other forms of out-of-home media that are not being utilized. The media company would rather make a little money selling a sign to you at a bargain rate, than leaving the media vehicle vacant or with an old, non-paying client reaping the rewards of free advertising.

Consider these other out-of-home options. Some of them include elements of events and print, but they won't cost you an arm and a leg:

- Sponsor an athletic event such as a 5K run. Typically, you will get a table, distribution of you business information in a "sponsor gift bag" and some signage.

- Create a flyer. Post it and distribute it wherever it is legally permitted. Posting in colleges, supermarkets, "mom & pop" storefronts, etc. can get the word out very inexpensively. Distribution of flyers can range from house-to-house to standing in a single high traffic location and handing them to passers-by. You can hire college students to help keep costs down or hire professionals who can guarantee a greater degree of success through various techniques they employ.

- Set up a table at the local fitness center/gym. Many establishments will allow you to rent some space at the front entrance where you can distribute literature, maybe include a special offer, and explain your unique selling proposition.

- Place advertising on your car. "Moving billboards" are well read and memorable. You do not have to turn your personal property into a "circus" to promote your business. Custom magnetic signs that you can easily mount and remove are the solution to advertising your business only when you want to. Again, follow the rule-of-thumb for outdoor signage: keep the message short. Provide the company name;

state what the business does, if it is not implied in the name; list a telephone number and your company's website address.

• Rent a table/booth at local places of worship. Many churches, synagogues, etc. host various events and offer local businesses inexpensive sponsorship opportunities.

• Distribute balloons with your company's name, services, phone number and URL at events, charities, parties, parks, etc. Printing will typically cost between 5 and 20 cents per balloon depending on whether there is one-sided or two-sided messaging, size of balloon, number/type of colors used.

• Distribute bookmarks with your company information. Of course, you must make sure your local library, bookstores, card shops, etc. will accept them and leave them in conspicuous places for consumers to happily take them home for free. You can put a substantial amount of information on bookmarks, so consider offering a discount, contest or promotion that drives people to call you or register on your website.

• Tee shirts, polo shirts and baseball caps with printed or embroidered messages are all wonderful ways of staying in front of potential customers. These forms offer some of the least expensive means of "reminder" advertising available. A quality-printed tee shirt will last a long time. Not only does it remind the original recipient of the shirt, who and where he/she received the "gift" from, but it sends a message to others every time it is worn. Some of these items are so cherished that they outlive the companies whose products and services they promote.

• College campuses can be a very attractive venue, if your product lends itself to teens and young adults. Check to see if universities in the area allow vendors to set-up tables at events. You may be allowed to post a small sign in the student union building or cafeteria. Leaflets may also be permitted.

There are also professional companies that can recommend various types of college-oriented media to you.

• Medical practices may offer inexpensive media opportunities. Perhaps you know a doctor who does not offer enough reading material in the waiting room. Suggest to the doctor that your business "sponsor" a magazine rack. If the doctor doesn't already have a rack, you purchase an inexpensive rack and, in exchange, your business gets exclusive category rights to distribute its literature in the racks. Your information will garner a higher level of credibility when it sits among publications such as National Geographic, Time, Newsweek, WebMD Magazine and important medical literature.

There are so many forms and variations of Out-of-home advertising that you could easily write a 500-page book on this medium alone. Suffice it to say that as you walk around outside or as you visit places outside of your home become attuned to what advertising is present. You will probably come up with a few inexpensive ideas of your own.

6. Internet - This has rapidly changed the face of business and literally the way we live our lives. You already know this and you are also aware that it continues to evolve at such a rapid pace that it is very difficult to keep up with all of it. Don't fret and don't try to keep up with everything because you can't. What you can do is look at the big picture, talk to some of the real pros and trendsetters that you may know or have access to and, occasionally, attend a webinar. Webinars are great for small businesses because you can attend them without leaving your office. Equally as important, many of them are free. So, you can learn a great deal about the Internet and the latest trends while you save time and money. Learning should be on going because the Internet and the next great "wave", Mobile computing, must be built into your business operations. If you do not embrace the Internet and Mobile communications you place the survival of your business in great peril.

Think of Mobile as the ability to do everything from watching TV to listening to the radio, to searching the Internet, to getting and sending email, and conducting much of your social and business activity without the need to be stationary. You can be on the go, traveling from one place to another and multi-tasking to your heart's content. Currently, the only thing holding Mobile back is adoption. With the advent of larger screen sizes (IPad), more tools and programs (apps and browser access/compatibility) and consumer understanding and acceptance, Mobile is a very big part of the future of business.

Regarding the Internet, here are some of the things that you must do as soon as humanly possible, if you haven't already implemented them:

• Website – If you do not have one, make it your first order of business. Actually, the first step is to choose and purchase a Web address (URL). Don't even print business cards until you have a URL and an individual business email address for yourself and any other key people in your company. Certain businesses try to get by with Google, Yahoo or an AOL address, but that sends a signal that your business is home-based or, worse-yet, part-time and "less than professional".

There are reputable companies that can design your website for as little as $500. This is an area where it can really pay off to shop around. A $500 website may suffice for the moment, but it may not serve you well enough if you experience the growth that you hope for. It may only cost you an additional $1,000 to $2,000 to get a significantly better website that makes a "big" statement about your services and leads to far more sales.

• **Search Engine Optimization (SEO)** – Unlike the movie, "Field of Dreams", you cannot simply build your website and have potential customers come in droves. Marketing your website is important if you want to generate leads from potential customers performing online searches. SEO is one of the least costly means at your disposal. I know marketers who do SEO for themselves. If you do not have the time or the inclination to learn SEO and perform regular maintenance, there are many capable companies that specialize in this area.

• **Paid Search / Online lead-generation companies** – There are hundreds of companies in the business of acquiring and selling leads to businesses of all sizes in virtually every category you can think of. It is likely that you have used one or more of these, either as a consumer "shopping around" or as a business seeking new leads. Some of these companies are very well known such as AT&T YellowPages.com, SuperYellowPages.com, Service Magic, eLocal Listing, Merchant Circle, and, of course, Google, Yahoo and Bing.

Paid search is absolutely worth testing. You may prefer to do it yourself via a service such as Google Adwords or you may prefer something more turnkey, such as ReachLocal, a company that can plan and implement the program for you.

Here's the thing to keep in mind about Paid Search: you only pay when a potential customer clicks on your ad and visits your landing page and/or website. That visit may or may not generate a lead in the form of a phone call, contact-form completion or other means of capturing the potential customer's information. On the other hand, if you work with a lead generation company, they will supply you with leads.

The amount that you pay for a lead can vary greatly depending on which lead-generation company you use. For example, if you use YellowPages.com for telephone call leads, your cost-per-lead may be relatively high (e.g. $25.00) versus Service Magic.com (e.g. $15.00). However, you may find that the quality of the leads generated by YellowPages is superior and results in more sales than the leads from Service Magic. Again, the aforementioned is only a hypothetical example, not a recommendation. The point to bear in mind is that the quality of the lead is ultimately more important than the cost of the lead.

The most important thing to do with Paid Search and Lead Generation services is keep good records of the number of leads, cost per lead, number of sales and total amount of each sale generated, so that you can perform an on-going analysis and improvement of your online lead generating activities. You must have a "test and refine" mentality.

Social Media – The great thing about Social Media is that a small business can gain a significant presence for **free**. Three of the major Social Media, Facebook (a social networking site), Twitter (a microblog), and LinkedIn (a business-oriented social networking site) are a great starting point for most businesses. They are all free on the basic service level. YouTube, is another free marketing tool at your disposal. If you can develop videos that feature your business and will be of interest to potential customers or existing customers, than YouTube makes sense.

Many marketing experts feel that the aforementioned Social Media are not the most effective means of reaching the online community for free. There are those who argue that blogs, online reviews, forum threads, and a press and media campaign will garner better results. These are all excellent tools. Some are free, while others will require a budget to do them correctly. Let's face it, most small businesses don't have the time to do an effective Public Relations effort, nor would many know where to start. However, there are very capable writers and PR companies with reasonable rates ready to help small businesses.

Social Media is all the rage at the moment. Don't overreact to the hype and understand what SM can and cannot do for a small business. It is more suited to customer relationship management than it is to acquiring new customers. It is great for carrying on a dialogue with your existing customers. You can let them know about new services/products and special offers and coupons. You can engage them on a one-on-one basis and get great feedback from them. This will lead to product improvements and increased sales from existing customers because you have formed a more intimate bond with them. Let's face it, current and past customers are your best advocates if they like you. In this way, Social Media will indirectly lead to new customers.

7. Email – Opt-in email campaigns to current customers as well as efforts directed to potential customers via third-party lists have proven to be very effective. If your current customer base is small and you do not want to invest in purchasing an email list here are ways to build a list of your own:

- Link to a sign-up form that is on your Web site by including the link in your email signature line
- Promote your online sign-up page in your brochures and other sales collateral
- Conduct a contest or drawing to encourage people to sign up
- Put a newsletter subscription URL on the footer of catalogs or printed newsletters
- Feature the newsletter subscription URL on print ads or on bill stuffers
- Promote sign up via telephone messaging while on hold and voice mail

- Link to event registration, online donation to charities or any other activity that provides the opportunity to promote a sign-up
- Include a sign-up offer it in your shopping cart mechanism
- Create a face-to-face sign-up sheet at your store, events, trade shows or while networking
- Allow people to forward your communications to others via a "forward this newsletter to others" option in your email communication
- Promote the newsletter via Paid Search
- Use Search Engine Optimization to drive sign-ups
- Send direct mail highlighting the online discussion. Mention that you are offering some incentives or discounts via e-mail only
- Offer opt-in incentives - Discounts or access to white papers and/or special reports
- Hand out sign-up forms at speaking engagements and seminars
- Collect business cards with e-mails on them at trade show booths
- Make changing an email address easy. Try to allow for subscribers to update the address on their own
- Require an email address when people register for events

Ronald Hatcher

Ron Hatcher has over 30 years experience in marketing communications. He honed his skills in the media department of major agencies including Grey, McCann Erickson and NW Ayer (which is now MEC). In 1989, he was recruited to be the Media Director of Burkhardt & Christy, where he helped the agency to triple in size. In 1995, he formed his own agency, Munn Rabôt, with three other partners.

In 2008, Ron launched Vantage Point Media, a firm focused on providing businesses with highly strategic, effective and affordable media planning and buying. Ron's extensive brand experience, prior to founding Vantage Point Media, includes BMW Motorcycles, Goodyear Tires, Coca-Cola, AT&T, Bristol Myers, Revlon, R.J. Reynolds, McDonald's, Bahamas Ministry of Tourism, NewYork-Presbyterian Hospital, Oppenheimer, Sony, Nintendo, Smirnoff Vodka, Nestle and others.

He has managed the development and implementation of plans ranging from a single, local market to multi-national efforts.

Ron believes it takes more than buying efficiently to get the best results; it requires understanding the unique power of each medium and how the various media fit into the customer's everyday life.

He seeks to extend the impact of his client's marketing efforts by developing free (added-value) elements as well as paid sponsorships and events. Examples of this include negotiating the placement of BMW's motorcycle line in prime locations of the Hartsfield Atlanta International Airport for a two-year period leading up to, and including, the 1996 Olympics; developing and implementing a one-of-a-kind news-content "product placement" for Children's Hospital of New York-Presbyterian on WCBS-AM (880); arranging for the Goodyear blimp to be featured in a Latin American beauty pageant TV event which was viewed in over 15 countries; negotiating GHI's sponsorship and participation in the New York City Triathlon; and establishing Atlantis as the official health plan of the Mets Class A baseball team, the Brooklyn Cyclones.

Contact information:
Vantage Point Media, LLC
1202 Hillside Terrace
Pomona, NY 10970
Main office: 845-694-8686
Web address: www.vpm.us.com
Ron Hatcher, Founding Partner / CEO
Cell - 914-584-5576; email: r.hatcher@vpm.us.com

Mediation for Business Owners

By Robert J. McDonnell, MS APM

"Discourage litigation. Persuade your neighbors to compromise whenever you can."

- Abraham Lincoln

When a conflict or disagreement arises in business or business relationships, today's business owners are realizing that mediation can play a helpful role in resolving their situation. Whether the issue in dispute is a contract, an employer-employee relationship, or other matter, mediation is becoming popular as an easier, generally quicker, and less expensive way to move ahead.

That is, because…

- Parties maintain privacy and control over the outcome of the dispute
- The process is informal and inexpensive — attorneys may, or may not, be required to participate
- It is a non-adversarial approach
- The process encourages creative solutions
- Mediation can preserve and enhance relationships, while setting guidelines for future relationships
- Mediation eliminates magnification of disputes which often accompanies costly litigation

What is mediation?

Mediation is a process that provides for trained third party neutrals to facilitate communication and negotiation among parties in order to help resolve current and ongoing disputes. By helping parties change the quality of their conflict interaction from negative and destructive to positive and constructive, the mediator facilitates the parties to make their decisions together, based on an understanding of their own views, the other's views and the situation they face. Because mediation is non-adversarial, it is very different than litigation.

Mediation is rapidly becoming a popular and successful form of dispute resolution. Through the confidential process, individuals in conflict are provided with the opportunity to make better choices in the face of conflict and interpersonal differences, leading to more informed, satisfying and lasting resolutions. Not only can the actual dispute be resolved, but mediation offers the opportunity for the participants to overcome misunderstandings and misperceptions and to restore trust and respect in their working relationship. At the same time, the problem solving and negotiation skills applied, developed and learned in mediation can be used by participants to help resolve future disputes.

The most important prerequisite for a successful mediation is the willingness of the parties to resolve the disagreement. Mediation has a statistically high success rate and participants report greater satisfaction with the process and the outcome than in traditional litigation (including arbitration).

There are typically two main areas of business relationships where mediation works effectively. In the first, parties have a dispute and need to have financial resolution of the matter and move on separately. These instances involve positional bargaining where each party wants as large "a piece of the pie" as possible. The second is where there is an ongoing relationship and there will be business transactions or personal interactions in the future. These may include an employee/employer or supplier/client relationship, or possibly a business partnership.

In the situations where there is an ongoing relationship, mediation can be particularly beneficial. A mediator can assist with joint problem solving and help parties develop non-legal, more elegant, solutions for their mutual gain. Often, this aids in preserving the relationship.

Both individuals and businesses in litigation experience costs that are quite real, yet are often unseen. There are obvious costs associated with litigation, such as attorney costs, filing fees, depositions, discovery, etc. But there are also unseen costs that come with litigation, including lost productivity, time spent managing or participating in the various aspects of litigation, as well as emotional costs.

Basically, any dispute can be mediated, including those civil disputes involving contracts, leases, small business ownership, employment, and others. Non-violent criminal matters, such as claims of verbal or other personal harassment, can also be successfully mediated.

Although there are hundreds of thousands of laws on the books, many types of common disputes simply do not raise a legal claim that you can take to court. These can include disputes between family members, employees, or neighbors. Fortunately, mediation is available even when courts are not.

As an example, a successful family-owned business may be struggling with the issues that arise as the founder/owner looks to pass on ownership and/or control of the business. There may be varying levels of interest among the family members who feel they are entitled to, or expected to, come into ownership of the business. Mediation can provide the parties with a safe, non-threatening, process that would address the underlying interests and concerns of the parties and, with their agreement, assist the family in addressing the issues. Clearly, the family is interested in maintaining both the business and the family relationships, both of which could be negatively impacted by protracted adversarial litigation.

Understanding the process. What makes the process "mediation?"

Successful mediation, as an alternative method of dispute resolution, has the following elements:

1. An impartial third party

The third party neutral makes the entire process work. As long as there is a neutral facilitator, the parties can trust that they have safety in the process.

2. A third party who protects the integrity of the process.

Not only does the mediator not take sides against any party to the mediation, the mediator does not usurp the parties' rights to disclose, or not disclose information. The mediator preserves the integrity of the proceedings.

3. Good faith from the participants.

Good faith includes not only entering into mediation with the intent to work towards a resolution; it also includes not using the process for outside purposes. Both the behavior and integrity of the neutral are important in creating and preserving good faith.

4. The presence of the parties

Obviously, the parties to the dispute need to be present. Those with full authority to act for the parties must attend so that the parties can work towards resolution.

5. An appropriate site or venue

Generally this means a site that is conducive to the process. The location must be one where neutrality, confidentiality and inclusiveness can be maintained.

6. Confidentiality

In many states, the discussions during mediation sessions are confidential to the extent agree upon by the parties, or as provided for by other law or rule of the state. In most cases, parties expect that communications during mediation will not be discussed with others outside the mediation. Parties may even choose mediation to resolve the dispute to assure privacy of their issues.

Opting for Mediation —

Business owners in a dispute should consider suggesting mediation as a means for resolving the dispute. Parties in mediation have to agree to be there, so the first step is agreeing on a mediator. The parties can each provide proposed mediators and then mutually agree on the mediator.

Competent mediators come for a variety of professions and employ different styles. When choosing mediators, consider experience, reputation, training, profession, accreditation and/or certification. Consult with other business owners, attorneys, state ADR (Alternate Dispute Resolution) organizations, or state or national mediation organizations or associations.

Helpful advice for business owners in a conflict:

Don't litigate... mediate.

Robert McDonnell, MS APM

Robert J. McDonnell, MS APM, owner and principal of Alliance Mediation Services, has been formally practicing mediation since 2003 and brings to his practice over thirty years of experience in the telecommunication industry, focused primarily on regulatory policy development and issue resolution.

He served as President – New Jersey Association of Professional Mediators (NJAPM), from October 2008 through September 2010. He currently serves on the NJAPM Board as Immediate Past President.

Robert is an Accredited Professional Mediator (APM) and received accreditation from the New Jersey Association of Professional Mediators. His practice includes both civil and family mediation services in New Jersey. He has also been accredited as an Advanced Mediator Practitioner by the Association of Conflict Resolution. Robert was trained in mediation and dispute resolution at Rutgers University, where he received a Graduate Certificate in Conflict Management. He holds a Masters of Science degree in Engineering Management and a Bachelor of Science in Electrical Engineering, and also attended graduate policy programs at Stanford and the University of Michigan.

Robert is approved by the New Jersey Administrative Office of the Courts (AOC) for the Presumptive Mediation Program for Civil, General Equity and Probate Cases and mediates civil cases for the AOC in several counties in Northern New Jersey. He is also on the New Jersey AOC Roster of Foreclosure Mediators. He volunteers his mediation services and serves as a mediator for the municipal courts in Essex, Morris and Passaic Counties.

He is also an arbitrator, and participates on the Financial Industry Regulatory Authority (FINRA) panels in New York and New Jersey.

Robert J. McDonnell, MS APM
Accredited Professional Mediator
Alliance Mediation Services
39 Alpine Drive
P.O. Box 87
Lincoln Park, NJ 07035-0087
Tel: 973 709-0188
Fax: 973 709-0255
rmcdonnell@alliance-mediation.com
www.alliance-mediation.com

Merchant Services — Understand Their Costs And Use To Get New Clients

by Frank Gallipoli

Paying by plastic has become part of our everyday lives. Whether by credit card, debit EBT, gift cards or simply taking money out of the ATM, society has grown accustomed to carrying any of these. Today even businesses and government agencies issue cards to their employees as a method of payment to simplify accounting. Most banks issue some sort of check or debit card immediately upon opening a checking or savings account.

Sales and cash flow are two of the most important issues that business owners must constantly address. How do I attract more customers to buy my product or use my services? Equally as important if not more important is how do I get paid for my services rendered, products sold or both? In comes Visa, Mastercard, Discover, American Express, etc. to present their services.

The first question that a business owner must ask him or herself is, "Will this method of accepting payment be beneficial to the company?" More specifically, will this help increase sales and assist with the cash flow? This question can only be answered if the owner truly understands the companies targeted clients and how those clients prefer to pay. In most cases, the answer is an obvious yes.

If the answer to the first question is yes, then the next question that must be answered is, "How do you plan on processing the payments?" This is known as the method of capture. Today cards can be both swiped or manually keyed in. Checks can be scanned and guaranteed without even going to the bank. And customers can even shop and purchase items at 3AM through the merchants' e-commerce site. This will ultimately determine what type of equipment and/or software will be purchased, loaned or leased to the business. Different merchant service providers have a variety of equipment programs available. It is very important to inquire about these programs and the costs upfront.

You have decided that electronic payments will work for your company and the method of capture has been determined. Your next step is the difficult choice of choosing the merchant service provider that will work best with the way your company operates. This should include but not be limited to the overall customer service, technical support and how easy it is to reach and work with the customer service and technical support teams and finally, how responsive they are. Does the company provide a designated sales representative and if so, how accessible is this representative? Are contracts required? If so, for how long and what penalties would be enforced if the contract is broken? Are gift and loyalty programs also offered? Is the company accredited or affiliated with any reputable associations? What, if any, are the other miscellaneous fees (statement, service and PCI)? Last, but certainly not least, what kind of pricing programs does the company offer?

Before choosing the company based solely on "rate", it is important that you first understand how and for what the business is being charged when accepting any type of card. You will incur fees with this service, however, knowing why is very important. The pricing system that rates are based upon is extremely complex. Shopping for the lowest introduction rate does not necessarily mean that you will have received the best overall deal for your company. The fact is that it could cost the business hundreds, if not thousands, of dollars annually or even monthly if the merchant neglects to look at the all of the possible charges that can and will be incurred. Beware of the representative who only tries to sell the lowest rate!

Merchant service card transactions are cleared and settled by acquiring banks with the issuing banks through a system called Interchange. The system also regulates the rates and fees for the different types of cards that customers carry. These rates and fees are set by Visa or Master Card for all merchant service providers to base their pricing. The best way to explain this is by comparing the rate for a debit or check card issued by a bank that is used as a Visa or Mastercard during a purchase to a special rewards card that someone might be using to accumulate extra bonus miles to redeem for free or discounted items. Customers will use these cards and it is virtually impossible for the merchant to know what type of card is being presented until your statement is received. It is equally as important to understand that keyed in transactions or e-commerce transactions will be charged at a higher cost based on this same Interchange price structure.

Imagine the following example. Using simple math, a $100 purchase at a retail store that might only cost the merchant $1.50 if a debit or check card is used could cost more than $5.00 in some cases, depending on what pricing program the business chose, if a rewards card is used for that exact same purchase. If that same purchase is done via the Internet or is keyed in, the merchant might pay $2.75 for one type of card or more than $5.00 in some cases, again depending on which price program the merchant accepted for another card. These additional charges are typically known as Mid-Qualified transactions and Non-Qualified transactions.

Remember that the card companies are constantly advertising and marketing to consumers to obtain and use their cards when they purchase rather than using cash or a check. Having the logos in the window, counter, flyer, website, etc. helps attract consumers. Accepting cards as a method of payment reduces dealing with receivables 30, 60, 90, 120 days old. Promoting gift cards allows your company to receive payment prior to even selling the goods and services by providing certain incentives. Promoting loyalty cards help to entice consumers to purchase more of your product on a regular basis. Both provide additional marketing and company brand recognition that will help increase your customer base as well as help retain existing customers. Government benefits are paid by issuing EBT cards in lieu of paper checks and food stamps.

As shown, there is much more than meets the eyes with this complicated pricing structure. Understand exactly how your business will be capturing the payments and who your customers are. Talk to your representative about all of the services, not just the price structure. Make sure that charges will be clearly identified in the monthly statements. Don't be afraid to ask these questions. Most importantly, grow your business by concentrating on what you do best without fear of the merchant service providers invoices, knowing that you have successfully addressed the items in this chapter.

Alternative Business Financing – Bridge Your Financial Gap

by Frank Gallipoli

Alternative financing might just be the most misunderstood phrase in lending among borrowers. Simply put, the phrase is used most often when conforming financing cannot be obtained through traditional means such as conventional bank lending programs. This would include how quickly the funds are required. Although many alternative financing programs, specifically sub-prime lending, have disappeared over the years due to the predatory lending laws, there are still many good financing options available for business owners. Whether there is a thriving or a downturn in the economy, these programs have been around for many years and can be of great assistance for business owners depending on the situation.

Forms of alternative lending can include; asset based lending such as accounts receivable financing also known as factoring programs, inventory and purchase order financing, cash flow loans or merchant cash advance. Private and angel investors will also lend money for a specific business type or property. Choosing the program that works best for the business will depend mostly on broker funding resources, the business owners due diligence or both. It is important to understand all of the details of the financing program and exactly how it can and will benefit the business. The dumb question is the one that is not asked!

Historically small businesses have always struggled to secure conventional bank financing loans. At times, being declined for a loan can be a degrading and humiliating experience. There are many different reasons why going the alternative financing route might in some circumstances be more advantageous to the business owner. Be it preference or necessity, funding terms, funding times, personal guarantees, amount required, credit issues, collateral, length of time in business, terms or convenience, are just a few reasons why this might be a better method of obtaining financing.

Interest rates are typically higher than what local banks will offer as core or introductory pricing products. On the flipside, underwriting guidelines and criteria are often much more flexible and easier for business owners to work with. Additionally, projects and loans can be funded in a much faster time period as well, sometimes in as little as two business days. Some programs will allow monthly interest only payments to be made over a specific period of time, while other programs will fully amortize the loan. Again, it is important to know all of the terms and conditions of the loan, including late payments and early payoff penalties, if any. Always make sure there is an exit strategy in place.

Utilizing these resources can benefit a business in many ways. For the most part, alternative lenders do not place restrictions on the use of funds. Business owners can utilize these programs for all different reasons. Many have outstanding receivable issues and need the working capital to meet payroll, expand inventory, pay debt or taxes, address emergency repairs, manage unexpected operating expenses, or expand or remodel the facility. Maybe the business wants to do some additional advertising and marketing to promote the company and products. Some are just trying to overcome seasonality or cyclicality. Others don't want to risk personal assets and prefer not to sign personal guarantees.

Unlike traditional lending, Alternative financing programs do not solely determine approvals based on credit scores, income and financials. These programs also factor into consideration many aspects of the business such as cash-flow volume, receivables, inventory, and the type of business making funds easier to obtain. Certain businesses that have recently been declined for a loan from a traditional lender might find funds readily available from an alternative source because of this.

These programs are not for everyone but can and have helped millions of businesses around the world achieve their goals. They can provide simple solutions to assist a business and should not be discounted. These programs will assist and address the specific monetary needs of the company allowing the owners to concentrate on running the business rather than worrying about keeping the doors open or slowing the business growth due to lack of financing.

Frank Gallipoli

Mr. Gallipoli is the National Sales Director of Bank Card Systems, Inc. in Rochelle Park, NJ. Mr. Gallipoli with almost 20 years experience in the finance industry, Frank joined Bank Card Systems to promote current financial products and cutting edge technologies available within the payment card industry for accepting credit cards. Mr. Gallipoli is also able to offer small business owners access to alternative financing options through his numerous business affiliations and relationships.

Frank takes a great deal of pride assisting people both in business and personally. He actively serves in: the Meadowlands Chamber of Commerce Small Business Council; New Jersey Chamber of Commerce; and supports the Mid-Bergen Rotary Club, Gift of Life 7490 & Interact Club with his wife and children.

Frank is available for your questions at: frank@bcspos.com

Office: 800-223-8603

Public Speaking Skills for Business Owners/Sales Professionals

by Marlene Waldock

You are asked to give a presentation or maybe just introduce yourself at a meeting. All of a sudden your mouth gets dry, your breathing gets shallow, your palms start to sweat and when you stand up, your knees feel weak. You open your mouth to speak and it sounds like someone else's voice. Sometimes you are not even sure of what you said.

Sound familiar? Speaking in public is the most fear inducing act. Most people would rather die than give a speech or make a presentation. But as business owners and professionals in today's environment, you must be able to present your ideas and your business in a variety of venues - to promote your business

Even there are those who have a natural ability to be public speakers, it is something that you can learn. There are two major facets to good presentations - the message and the delivery

Consider this - a seasoned presenter can overcome a bad speech, a bad presenter can destroy a good speech and a novice presenter must start with a speech/presentation that is easy to deliver.

To put "pop" into your presentation you must"

- Prepare yourself
- Organize the material
- Present is as a conversation.

It's an easy process.

1. Begin with the core idea

2. Create a strong opening and closing

3. Have a conversation with the audience.

What causes the most fear? That you will forget what you are supposed to say? That you will say something stupid? Or that you will stumble around trying to find the right words? You anticipate an outcome that is not going to happen.

First - no one in the audience expects you to be perfect. I am a 25-year veteran public speaker. I began my career in public speaking at an early age – doing how to pack your suitcase for a luggage manufacturer in my home town. I can tell you that the first time I gave the presentation I was petrified. I later went on to be a national training director for a fortune 100 company, where I presented a 4.5 Audio visual program - the first time I gave that presentation no one heard a word I said, and I had a microphone. I always tell my audiences that if I say something that they didn't understand, or if I say something that makes no sense – to please stop me. I tell them from the beginning that I am not perfect.

Secondly - when you follow this process your presentation will be very easy to deliver.

1. Prepare yourself - what is your message? Keep it simple!

Ask yourself these questions - why am I there, why is the audience there. What outcome am I seeking? What outcome are they seeking?

Then you must consider the following: time of day, other activities, is this an open presentation or mandatory, are they paying or is it free?

Your preparation is all about the audience. Your goal is to make them comfortable because:

~ They want you to be successful.

~ They want to learn something from you.

~ And they don't care if you are perfect.

2. Organize for ease of delivery.

First impressions count - capture the audience's attention - create an interesting/strong opening. Set the stage - why are you giving your presentation. What is the expected outcome – make it clear.

Rule of the 7's - 7 seconds to make an impression – 7 seconds to capture attention – 7 seconds to tell your story in introduction summary- if you lose the audience in the first few they won't pay attention to what you are trying to say.

There are a variety of openings from asking a question to making a profound statement and taping into the audiences emotions to stating a fact.

The audience is there to learn something - let them know that what you have to say is something of interest.

Closing - first in last out rule - create a strong closing - leave them with something to think about.

3. Have a conversation with the audience.

How you do you do that? Envision yourself talking to a friend. Have eye contact with everyone in the audience as though you are talking to them. When you focus on the audience you can't think about yourself. The presentation becomes passionate, informative and real.

Tell stories, paint a verbal picture. Speak from the heart and talk about that which you know well. To accomplish your goal you need only to have one to three points.

Before you close – ask for questions. Never and I mean never, close your presentation on a question from the audience. You want to have the last word.

Present - don't encumber yourself with a lot of powerpoint sides. In fact, unless you have some unbelievable pictures to support your points, don't use powerpoint at all. There is nothing worse than a slide with a bunch of words on it. They came to hear you speak not to read what you have to say.

This is all about you. It's time to "pop."

Marlene J. Waldock

Marlene J. Waldock owns 1st Impression Communications, a results-directed communication strategies and solutions company with a focus on communication and presentation skills, founded in 1987. A nationally published writer and seasoned public speaker, for five years she was the host of a weekly TV program, NJ Business, seen on News 12 New Jersey reaching 1.7 million households in the state. In 2003 she was awarded The Small Business Administration (SBA) Journalist of the year Award for her work. From 2006 to 2009, as a member of the Board of Contributors for NJBIZ, a weekly business publication, she wrote quarterly editorials on topics pertinent to the business community. She has also authored articles in Family Circle Magazine on Powerful Communication Skills for Women, reaching 22 million readers world-wide.

Perhaps her greatest accomplishment, professionally and personally, is the creation in and ultimate success of "Because We Are Women: Celebrating Possibilities symposium. BWAW is an empowering experience that energizes, inspires, and supports personal growth, life achievement, and internal fulfillment. Since 2004, BWAW has touched hundreds of women, helping them to step into their power and live their dreams. In 1995, she became a member of The New Jersey Association of Women Business Owners (NJAWBO) and served as state president in 2003/2004. Just prior to becoming president, the Association honored her when they selected her BUSINESS WOMAN OF THE YEAR.

Ms. Waldock is very involved in the community. She is the president of the North Essex Chamber of Commerce, and sits on the board for Programs for Parents, and the Advisory Board for the Turnaround Management Association. Additionally, for three years, she participated in the PSEG supplier Diversity Council, promoting the viability of WBE and MBE as suppliers to Corporate America.

Marlene Waldock
first@1stimpressioncom.com
973-498-0046

Cash Flow Tips For Your Business

by Vito Mazza
Senior Consultant
GREENFlag Profit Recovery

When a company provides a product or service, it has every right to expect to be paid on a timely basis. However, anyone who's been in business a month or more has learned that prompt payment is not always the case. While customers and clients expect promptness and professionalism in regard to delivery of our products or services, somehow, they don't always adopt those same standards when it comes time to paying their bills!

Particularly in this economy, all businesses are interested in cutting costs and IMPROVING CASH FLOW!

Accounts not paid within your terms can have a dramatically negative impact on your "cash flow." We have all witnessed recently that the very survival of many businesses has been placed in jeopardy over this very issue.

1. Have a Defined Credit or Collection Policy

One of the major causes of overdue receivables is that the business has not explained to its customers and staff exactly when accounts are supposed to be paid. If customers are not clearly informed that their accounts are to be paid on time, then chances are they'll pay late or sometimes, not at all. Make sure that your terms of payment are clearly stated in writing to each customer. Being specific is very important. We encourage clients to use the concept of a "date certain" when talking about due dates and time. Instead of talking about payments being due in "10 Days" or "30 Days," give the actual date of July 9, 2011... the "date certain" so they don't have to figure out when 10 days or 30 days might actually be. Be diplomatic, but be persistent.

2. Invoice Promptly and Send Statements Regularly

If you don't have a systematic invoicing and billing system, get one. Many times the customer hasn't paid simply because they haven't been billed or reminded to pay in a timely manner. This situation usually occurs in smaller or newer businesses, where they may be short-handed on staff needed for timely invoicing and billing. If you don't have a systematic billing system, get one.

(FYI: Our Online Client Portal at GREENFlag has a FREE interface with QUICKBOOKS. Let us know the software you are using and maybe we already have an interface, or we can connect with your software provider to build an interface!) See #3

3. "Address Service Requested"

One of the most difficult collection problems is tracking down a customer who has "skipped." All businesses should be aware of a special service offered by the US Postal Service. Any statement or correspondence sent out from a business or professional office should have the words "Address Service Requested" printed or stamped on the envelope, typically just below your return address in the top left corner. If a statement or invoice is sent to a customer who has moved without informing you of their new address, and the words "Address Service Requested" appear on the envelope, the Post Office will research this information and return the envelope to you on a yellow sticker that gives the new address or other updated information. If the customer has placed a "forwarding order" with the Post Office, the Post Office is required to forward the envelope to the customer and give you a form #3547 with the new address. Currently, your business will be charged $0.50 per manual notice issued, a reasonable price to pay for your first level of "skip-tracing." This will keep your address files up to date.

Some software programs and CRM systems are able to capture this information digitally from The USPS. (FYI: our Online Client Portal at GREENFlag has that capability and issues reports to allow our clients to update client and debtor records.)

4. Contact Overdue Accounts More Frequently

There is no law that says that you may only contact a customer once a month. The old adage "The squeaky wheel gets the grease" has a great deal of merit when it comes to collecting past due accounts. It's an excellent idea to contact late payers every 10-14 days. Doing so will enable you to diplomatically remind the customer of your originally stated terms of payment.

(FYI: our Online Client Portal at GREENFlag has the capability to allow our clients to contact debtors every 21, 14, 10 or even 7 days, depending on the industry)

5. Use Your Aging Summary Report, Not your Feelings

Many well-meaning businesses owners (or staff members) have let an account age beyond the point of ever being collected because of the "feeling" that the customer would pay eventually. While there are isolated cases of unusual situations, the truth is that if you aren't being paid, someone else is. Stick to your systematic follow-up plan. You'll soon identify who really intends to pay and who doesn't. You can then take appropriate actions.

6. Make Sure Your Staff is Well-Trained

Even "experienced" staff members can sometimes become jaded when dealing with past due customers. This usually happens when debtors have broken promises for payment that have been made previously. Make sure the staff is firm, yet courteous when dealing with them. Your entire staff could benefit from customer service training because, in effect, they must "sell" your customers on the idea that you expect to be paid. Make sure that your collection staff is trained to both, bring the account to current status, while at the same time, maintaining "good will" with your client base.

Mini-Course on "HOW TO ASK FOR MONEY"

Asking For Money is a 3-Step Process!

Step One – Sympathize & Show compassion, "I know how that happens sometimes"

This diffuses any possible anger and may even catch them off guard.

Step Two – Restate the Obligation

"Mr. Smith, you know that your account was originally due on mm/dd/yyyy."

This should cause some guilt on their behalf as well as have them realize you are "right" in asking to be paid.

DO NOT ASK:

- How much can you pay?
- When can you pay?
- Can you pay something?

These questions give control of the conversation to the debtor, enabling them to give unreasonable answers

Step Three – "How Much Are You Short?"

"Mr. Smith, of the $200 that is owed, how much are you short, right now?"

1. If they can pay some of the amount due now, then give them a "date certain" to pay the balance.

2. If they are short the whole amount, you can still be in control to negotiate payment terms.

7. Admit any Mistakes on Your Part and correct them ASAP

Sometimes customers don't pay because they feel that you've made a mistake. If you have made a mistake, admit it and correct it quickly. Beware: Do not try and cover up mistakes!

Your customer realizes that mistakes can happen in business. Unfortunately, in today's difficult financial environment, many customers believe that as the owner or president, you "don't need the money." Denying an obvious error only fans the fire of resentment that many of your customers may already be feeling today.

8. Follow all Federal (FDCPA) and State Collection Laws

Check out THE FAIR DEBT COLLECTION PRACTICES ACT, revised in (2006) on the web at: http://www.ftc.gov/bcp/edu/pubs/consumer/credit/cre27.pdf .

In many states, businesses are governed by the same collection laws that regulate collection agencies. For example, calling customers at an odd hour or disclosing to a third party that the debtor owes you money, are just a couple of the numerous collection practices that can cause serious repercussions. If you're not sure, call your state's department of finance which governs and monitors collection agencies.

9. Use a Third Party Sooner

If you've systematically pursued your past due accounts for 60 to 90 days from the due date, (and they still haven't paid) you're being delivered a message by your client. More than likely, you've requested payment four to six times in the form of phone calls, letters and statements. Statistics show that after 90 days, in-house collection efforts lose up to 80% of their effectiveness. That means that the time and financial resources budgeted for "in-house" collection efforts should be focused within the 1st 60-90 days, when the bulk of your accounts can and should be collected.

From that point on, a 3rd party can motivate your clients to pay you in ways that your staff simply can not, based solely upon the fact that the demand for payment is coming from someone other than you or your in-house (1st PARTY) team. This is called the "POWER of 3rd PARTY INTERVENTION".

When to Seek a 3rd Party

- According to written policies/procedures
- Broken promises – "check is in the mail"
- Unable to reach by phone (voicemail, in a meeting, answering service, etc.)
- Disconnected Phone or Number changed to unlisted
- Missed Payments, Payments getting smaller
- Certified mail returned "Unclaimed"
- Admission of inability to pay
- Debtor says "You'll get paid when I get paid"
- Bounced Check and no response
- Disputed Balance, disputed quality of service or product

Before paying a contingency collection agency, an attorney or using small claims court, why not explore the option using "EARLY, DIPLOMATIC, 3RD PARTY INTERVENTION" for a fixed flat-fee?

10. Remember that Nobody Collects Every Account

Even by setting up and adhering to a specific collection plan, there will still be a few accounts that will never be collected. By identifying these accounts early, you will save yourself and your company a great deal of time and money. Even though a few may slip by, you'll find that overall the number of slow pay and nonpaying accounts will greatly diminish, and that's a victory in itself!

Vito Mazza

Mr. Mazza holds a BA in English in Secondary Education from New Jersey City University in Jersey City, New Jersey. Upon graduation Mr. Mazza started his 28 year career with World Book Education Products. He began this career working in the products division as a part time teacher's product representative and then worked his way through the management levels to Distributor level where he became the president of his own company called Parental Partners, Inc. Vito has also travelled and trained in Canada, India and Russia on behalf of World Book International. In 2002, Mr. Mazza took all of his robust business experience, and joined GreenFlag by Transworld Systems, Inc. as The District Manager of the Manhattan Office, which he lead for 5 years. He is currently a Senior Consultant, working out of the NEW YORK METRO Office in NJ, where he is assisting Business Owners & Medical Practices with their CASH FLOW Management needs.

He is available to present a FREE Seminar to business groups, Chambers or Rotary Clubs, or Physicians Study Groups based on these Cash Flow Tips!

Vito Mazza
Senior Consultant
GreenFlag
Transworld Systems, Inc.
800-850-5110
201-446-4072
vito.mazza@TransworldSystems.com
http://web.transworldsystems.com/manhattan/

W2 Or 1099 – The Wrong Choice Can Cost You Your Business

by James Hyland

You are running your business and you need to grow and hire help but you want to eliminate liability and minimize your headaches, so you tell your new hires that they will be 1099 independent contractors… smart idea, right? WRONG!

First, we need to address the correct definition of what is a true 1099 Independent contractor. It is wholly you're responsibly to determine if the person providing you service is a true independent contractor or an employee. The IRS, will not give you any guidance, except for some general definitions, until after it is too late. The IRS will only give you guidance after the fact, which can be determined through an IRS or state labor audit or a worker's claim. A worker can complain that they were mis-classifed because they are seeking one of a few possible complaints against you or your company such as; that they want you to pay the employer side of taxes; or perhaps, seeking unemployment or disability benefits (an example is pregnancy) or workman's comp benefits. *Any of these or other possible aspects a worker can complain to the state or the federal department of labor which can result in fines and penalties for mis-classification and potential tax liability exposure.* As an example of the tax liability is being held responsible for the taxes you didn't collect from the employee, the employee's portion of the taxes if they failed to pay them because you, as a company, are a government appointed collection agent. Also, penalties on any and all taxes on the aforementioned *because your payment are now late*. Also, fines can be levied for mis-classification of a worker's status. The end result of paying in cash, is the same as when you mis-classify an independent contractor, which includes the fines and penalties, etc.

IRS definitions of:

1099 Independent Contractor:

~ A person operating their own business or trade that offer their services to the public or other companies. The determining factors of what makes a sub contractor, it is defined by the varying levels of control. There are three common rules which all must be met.

1) Who is in control the work and the worker? Aspects such as: time tables and controlling the standard of how the work is completed. Other aspects may include: where to purchase materials and who to hire, as in sub-contractors, where and when to purchase supplies for the job as in quality of supplies and materials.

2) Who is in control of the financial aspects? Such as: time tables for payment and who sets the rate payment and whose tools and supplies are being used. For true contractors there must be opportunities for profit and loss.

3) Type of relationship? Aspects such as the contractors business must exist without this job. They must have other opportunities; they must invoice (on letterhead with company address and phone number) for their work; they must have a business card and business phone number. They must have a contract stating how this work was paid for under the contractors terms. Contractors are paid by contracted hourly rate or by the job where employees are paid weekly or hourly. Defined by contracted job not indefinitely. *If there is a permanency to the work on a full time basis then that going into and under category of W2 employee.* Can the contractor prove that he has the available time to work for others?

W2 Employee:

~ There are 3 types of employees:

1) Someone who works under your control and direction in your work environment. How many days worked and how many hours per day worked as well as compensation are all established by the business owner.

2) Statutory Employee is basically someone who could qualify as an independent contractor under the first set of employee rules but may be treated by as an employee for tax purposes. They must meet certain conditions that all the work is to be primarily performed by them personally and they do not have a substantial investment in tools used to perform the tasks. The services are performed on a continuous basis on a year round basis.

3) Statutory non-employee – Only works for the one company but the employee controls their own hours and services are performed under contract. This is most common in sales organizations such as real estate sales, *where the broker tells the agent that the agent cannot work for any other agency* but the agent can dictate most of their own work details.

In summary, if you have a temporary need, the most intelligent course of action is to utilize the services of a temporary employment agency which removes the burden from you, the business owner, as to the classification of the worker and the liability for filing taxes for the employee as well as any potential future unemployment and disability claims as well.

If your needs are more long term, protect your business and tread very carefully.

James Hyland

James Hyland is a graduate from Seton Hall and Upsala Universities. After an extensive career in corporate America, Jim started ASA Payroll in 1990. He sought to give northern New Jersey small business owners an better alternative to the payroll giants. Mr. Hyland's approach includes highly detailed customer service and always being able to give not just more competitive pricing but also provide extensive knowledge and council on a variety of business topics to assist his clients. Mr. Hyland is an expert on IRS and state payroll issues as well and has many times come to the aid of his clients when he has noticed them making a possibility detrimental business maneuver in how they categorize their employees. He has saved many a small business owner from heavy fines and penalties from the IRS through his quick actions and eye for detail. Many of his clients have noticed and appreciated that if they had stayed with a typical payroll giant they could have been tied up in intrusive and lengthily IRS and state investigations had Mr. Hyland not caught and corrected the innocent mistakes.

James Hyland
President
ASA Payroll
West Milford, New Jersey
973-728-0433
jhyland@asapayroll.com
www.asapayroll.com

SECTION 4

Critical Information For Those Facing Divorce

What To Do When Your Spouse Says "I'm Out of Here!"

by Carolyn N. Daly, Esq.

Your spouse has announced that they want a divorce. First, don't panic and, although you inevitably will from time to time, try not to react out of emotion. Take some time and digest what you just heard. Then, make sure that there really will be a divorce. Talk to your spouse, if you can; see a qualified therapist, if necessary. People are often shocked to hear a divorce lawyer say that, but going through the process of divorce, and remember it is a process, can be time consuming, emotionally difficult and financially draining. Therefore, you want to be sure it is the right decision.

If your spouse has moved out of the house with little or no warning and cleared out your bank accounts, or taken the children with them, then you may not have the luxury of considering your options and should get to an attorney quickly. However, if there is no rush and the two of you have some time to consider the decision, then the following are some things that you should or should not do to afford you some protection while the decision is being made:

1. Consult with an attorney. You do not necessarily have to retain one at this point, but it is good to have a consultation so that you know what your options are. This is often the best money spent in a divorce.

2. Do not incur any additional debt. Do not sign a home equity loan. Do not sign any business loans. Do not plan any extravagant vacations for which you will go into debt.

3. Do not enter into a contract to buy a new house.

4. Do not sign anything else at the request of your spouse. Review it with an attorney first.

5. Do not liquidate any large assets.

6. If you are not in the habit, start making copies of financial records.

7. If the family finances are maintained on Quicken or a similar personal finance computer program, either print out the records or make a digital copy.

8. Establish credit in your own name. It is easier to obtain credit in your own name prior to a divorce being filed.

9. If you have received any inheritance or gift (other than from your spouse), do not commingle it with marital monies. Keep it segregated and intact. You may need it in the event of separation.

10. Open an account in your own name in a bank where you do not have jointly held accounts and where neither of you does business. It may be advisable to withdraw half the funds from joint liquid accounts, i.e. bank accounts, and to deposit them in an account you hold in your own name, understanding you are fully accountable for the removal of such funds. You may also need to set aside monies for emergencies and to have funds available for such things as retainers to attorneys, expert's fees, etc.

11. Start keeping track of relevant events, including absences from the home by the spouse, yourself and\or exercise of parenting time\visitation, if applicable. Record dates, times and explanations.

12. Make sure your automobile is in good working condition and has serviceable tires. You should also check the title to see that it is titled in your name or joint names.

13. Undergo necessary medical treatments, so long as they are covered under medical insurance.

14. Keep a low profile. Do not get into verbal or physical altercations. Walk away if necessary.

Once there has been a decision made to divorce, the next question is how to proceed. If you and your spouse are on speaking terms, and fairly amicable then you should consider mediation. Mediation is a process by which you and your spouse meet with a trained, neutral professional, typically a lawyer or mental health professional, to help you resolve all of the issues relating to the divorce. A mediator does not represent either of you, but assists you and your spouse in reaching your own resolution of the issues. It is generally not binding on either of you until a formal agreement is prepared and signed by both of you. Typically parties hire an attorney to advise them during the mediation process. Your attorney can, but is not always required to attend mediation sessions with you which can also help keep expenses down. Mediation is often less expensive and less adversarial than traditional divorce litigation making it attractive to many. However, both of you have to be prepared to communicate and to be cooperative to make mediation effective.

So, mediation sounds good, but having considered it, you determine that it simply will not work for you and your spouse. Before you run to court, there is another option to resolve your issues outside of divorce; arbitration. Arbitration is a process by which you and your spouse agree, essentially, to hire a trained, neutral professional, or professionals, to serve as your private judge or judges and decide the issues. Again, an arbitrator doesn't represent either you or your spouse and the process is conducted much like a trial. Therefore, each of you will probably have hired an attorney to represent you in the process. Witnesses can be called and documents and other evidence produced. The benefit of arbitration is that it typically results in a faster resolution and can be cheaper than traditional litigation. Another benefit is that once the arbitrator has rendered a decision, their decision is final and subject to review by a court under very limited circumstances. This means that you and your spouse will have some finality at the end of the process instead of having to face potential appeals and repeated visits to court in the future.

Another option to resolve your issues without court intervention is Collaborative Divorce. Collaborative Divorce has been around for some time, but has been gaining popularity in many states in recent years. In Collaborative Divorce, each of you will hire an attorney, but the attorney's role is that of negotiator, and not litigator. It is a non-adversarial process and the goal is to reach a settlement. Depending upon the issues and their complexity, you and your attorneys may agree to bring in other professionals, such as accountants, mental health professionals, financial experts, actuaries, etc. to help in resolving the issues. At the start of a Collaborative Divorce, you and your attorneys agree in writing to exchange all financial and relevant information, which is confidential to the process. This can cut down on the costs of obtaining relevant and necessary documents yourself. It also encourages disclosure of everything by each of you. You and your attorneys also agree in writing, typically in the same document, that should negotiations fail, each party will have to hire a new attorney to litigate the matter, starting from the beginning of the process. The belief is that this requirement keeps the parties focused on a settlement and provides a financial incentive to reaching a resolution.

What happens if none of the above methods to resolve your case will work? Then you are left with resolving the matter in court. You should retain an attorney to represent you. There are many ways to find an attorney. You can ask friends and colleagues for recommendations. You can call your state or local bar and ask if they have a lawyer referral service. You can Google for an attorney. Once you have some names, I suggest that you go for a consultation with some, or all of them, so that you can decide if they are the right fit for you.

Do they understand the issues you are facing? Does their view of the case match yours? How do they communicate with you? What are their hourly rates and billing practices? Will the partner be handling your case, or will it be an associate? The list of questions goes on, but it is important that you feel comfortable with the attorney you select to represent you. You should also consider hiring or consulting with an accountant, financial planner or psychologist to help you in resolving the economic and custody issues involved in your case. Your attorney is typically not qualified to provide tax advice, financial advice or mental health advice or support.

Then once you have decided which process is right for you, you need to decide what the issues are between you and your spouse that have to be resolved. In a typical divorce, the following issues are involved:

- Child(ren) custody: Legal and physical, including parenting time and visitation
- Child support; contribution to the children's education, college or private school
- Health and dental insurance for children, including uninsured or unreimbursed medical expenses
- Alimony (spousal support)
- Health insurance for you or your spouse (COBRA)
- Beneficiaries of life insurance policies
- Dividing property -- assets and debts
- Marital residence
- Vacation homes, time-shares.
- Businesses
- Retirement benefits (pensions, IRAs, 401(k) plans)
- Bank accounts

- Children's accounts -- custodial, savings, 529 plans
- Brokerage accounts -- stocks, bonds, and funds
- Stock options and restricted stock units
- Cars, boats, motorcycles, RVs, airplanes, etc.
- Home furnishings/collections/jewelry/family photos, etc.
- Airline miles and credit card points
- Debts
- Inheritances
- Tax consequences of the transfers of property pursuant to the settlement
- Tax deductions -- i.e. children as dependents, mortgage interest, real estate taxes, etc.
- Domestic violence concerns
- Resumption of maiden name (for women)
- Attorney's fees and expenses

This is a certainly not a comprehensive list of the issues that can be involved in resolving your case, but it is a good start. So, now that you know how you are going to resolve your case and what the issues are, what information and documents should you gather to provide to the attorney, or mediator, involved to help resolve these issues? The following is a list of preliminary documents / information that you should gather, bearing in mind that you may not be able to get all of them:

1. Copies of all federal, state and corporate tax returns for the last three years. Have a complete set of each, including all attachments and schedules.
2. A list of all assets (property) and liabilities (debts).
3. For every business involved and for which you or your

spouse has access to financial statements, provide the last three fiscal years' financial statements, all year-to-date financial statements, and the same periodic financial statements for the prior year (Quick Books records can be very helpful).

4. Copies of all insurance policies, including life, automobile, medical and umbrella policies.

5. Copies of the most recent statements for all credit cards or a list of all credit cards and obtain one year's statements for these accounts. If you don't know all of the credit card accounts, obtain a copy of your credit report. You can obtain one for free at www.annualcreditreport.com.

6. Copies of statements for all bank accounts for the last year, as well as copies of canceled checks.

7. Copies of statements for children's accounts.

8. A copy of the most recent documents identifying each employment benefit for you and your spouse, i.e. insurances, flexible spending accounts (FSAs), stock options, restricted stock units, etc.

9. Copies of plan documents for all pension plans, 401k plans, profit sharing plans, employee stock purchase plans, etc. Make copies of year end statements (these are usually generated between January and March of each year for every participant in the plan).

10. Copies of statements for all stock accounts and brokerage accounts.

11. Appraisals of property, whether real property or personal property. For personal property, you may have done an appraisal for a rider to your homeowner's insurance.

12. Copies of any loan applications.

13. Copies of financial statements or financial plans prepared by a professional.

14. An inventory of the contents of any jointly held safe deposit box, as well as household valuables such as silver, china, antiques, and art objects. Take pictures of valuable items so that you have a record of them in case they "disappear" before your matter is resolved.

15. A list of return addresses of all mail received by your spouse from brokerage houses, banks, insurance companies, credit cards so you can be sure that you didn't miss any assets or debts.

16. Documentation concerning income. For each income source in the current and prior calendar year, including income from employment, investment, government programs, gifts, trust distributions, prizes, and income from every other source, provide pay stubs, a current income statement, and the final income statement for the prior year; i.e. a W-2.

17. Documents that show average monthly expenses for your shelter, transportation and personal expenses, including employment related child care expenses, extracurricular activities, tutors, camps, private education, unreimbursed medical expenses, etc.

Again, this is not an exhaustive list of documents and information that will need to be gathered and provided, but it is a good start. Divorce is a stressful life event, even under the best of circumstances where you and your spouse get along. I hope that this brief overview of the process and things to consider when you are faced with a divorce will alleviate some of the anxiety and provide you with some ways to protect yourself in the event of a divorce.

Carolyn N. Daly, Esq.

Carolyn N. Daly, Esq. is a partner of Daly & Associates, LLC (www.dalyfamilylaw.net) in Morristown, New Jersey. She is a Certified Matrimonial Law Attorney and has been named a Super Lawyers, Rising Star from 2006 through 2010.*

Her prominent practice focuses on family law (divorce, alimony, college contribution, domestic violence, mediation, custody, parenting time, grandparents' rights, non-dissolution) and real estate law.

Ms. Daly prides herself on a pragmatic, no-nonsense approach to resolving family law matters. Ms. Daly's diverse background, focusing on family law after having practiced in several other areas. This diversity has helped Ms. Daly to identify issues that are often overlooked in family law.

An active member of the New Jersey State, Morris County and American Bar associations, Ms. Daly sits on the Morris County Child Support Partnership Committee. She regularly serves as an Early Settlement Panelist in Morris County.

Contact phone: 973-292-4700
cdaly@dalyfamilylaw.net
6 South Street, Suite 301
Morristown, NJ 07960

*No aspect of this advertisement has been approved by the New Jersey Supreme Court. For methodology of selection see http://www.superlawyers.com/about/selection_process.html

Divorce Mediation — A Practical Way To Lessen The Cost & Stress

by Robert J. McDonnell, MS APM

Why are so many couples choosing mediation as a means of resolving their separation, divorce, or post-divorce issues?

- *To avoid conflict and the bitterness that comes with these difficult issues -*

With high divorce rates, and very visible celebrity divorce disasters, divorcing couples want to move on with their lives and stay out of court.

- *To save time and money –*

Today's litigated divorces are time consuming and extremely expensive.

- *To focus on the children –*

Most parents agree that the children come first. In mediation, they develop ways to handle joint parenting, but as divorced or separated parents.

- *To maintain dignity –*

Mediation provides a process that is thoughtful and dignified. It can help parties end a long term marriage with respect.

- *To maintain privacy –*

Parties can keep issues of out court, and financial and custody issues can be resolved in a private setting.

What is Divorce Mediation?

Divorce mediation is a confidential and voluntary process where a neutral mediator guides you and your spouse through the negotiation of your separation or divorce in a cooperative, and non-adversarial, setting. The process results in a settlement that becomes the basis for the legally binding divorce agreement. This agreement is typically unsigned by the parties and is called the "Memorandum of Understanding."

Because the professional divorce mediator is impartial and unbiased, the process helps parties create a unique separation agreement that works for them as they plan for the future and, if children are involved, as they develop a joint parenting agreement that is in the best interests of the children.

Parties in mediation learn how to recognize and deal with differences, and learn to reach decisions regarding support, equitable division of property, and parenting arrangements. Those using mediation find that they often eliminate the court-imposed requirements and delays, and learn to deal with issues without becoming enemies.

It is generally agreed that divorcing couples are more likely to abide by agreements that they have made themselves, than by court-imposed orders. Mediated agreements have the greater degree of success going forward.

How Long Does Divorce Mediation Take? How Much Will Mediation Cost?

Every case is different (of course), but the average divorce mediation might take three to six, one and one-half or two-hour sessions, generally taking a month or two to complete the process. More complex cases can take several months to complete. The cost of the mediator may range from $2,000 to $6,000 in total from both parties for the typical number of sessions. The payment of fees for mediation should be discussed during mediation. The cost for each party's attorney for consulting and review of the agreements is in addition to these mediator costs.

Mediation is less expensive than a settlement negotiated by counsel, or a full-blown litigated divorce, either of which can be many multiple times higher than the mediation costs.

Do I Need a Lawyer During Mediation?

Legal advice is an important part of the mediation process. Mediation is not a substitute for advice of a qualified attorney. Both parties are encouraged to use independent legal counsel for continuing advice during the mediation, and for the legal review of the agreement (the Memorandum of Understanding) before it is signed, or before the attorneys prepare the Divorce Agreement for filing with the court. Legal advice should not come from the impartial mediator. Even when the mediator is an attorney, the mediator cannot give either party legal advice. Although divorcing couples can file court documents on their own, the use of a qualified lawyer is always good advice. Ask the mediator for suggestions for attorneys to help with the legal review and filing requirements.

My Case is Too Complex for Mediation. What if We Can't Agree on All Issues?

In complicated divorce situations, or with complex financial issues, parties in mediation frequently are advised to consult with outside experts, such as accountants, appraisers, financial planners, and other professionals during the process. The mediator can bring these experts into the process, and include their products and resources in the process.

In cases where the parties agree on all but one or two issues, the time and effort spent in mediation is not wasted. An agreement can be prepared that addresses all of the settled issues, and the parties can then go forward with litigation on the limited issues, or take time to think about the issue(s) and, possibly, return to mediation.

How Do I Know if Mediation is Right for Us?

If you think that mediation might be something you and your spouse are interested in, but are unsure if it's the right way to proceed, you might consider consulting with a mediator and trying it for a session or two to see how you feel about the experience. Ask questions about the process and your situation, and you should get helpful answers. Most mediators charge on an hourly basis, so this is an inexpensive way to find out about mediation and obtain some information about the process... and the mediator.

When is Mediation Not Suitable?

There are circumstances where mediation will not be appropriate for your situation. Parties should not participate in mediation where there is a history of emotional or physical abuse, where there is any history of domestic violence or child abuse, or when there is a restraining order in effect. Both parties need to have a sense of self awareness of their individual rights, and not be in a position where they feel forced to agree to terms that would not be in their best interests. For some couples, it may be appropriate to delay mediation until both parties are emotionally ready to participate. An experienced mediator will recognize if you are not ready for mediation and will advise you accordingly.

How Do I Get Started? Choosing a Mediator.

Couples facing divorce often panic and in the interest of protecting their finances, access to children, or for a myriad of other reasons, turn to litigation as a first step. If you think that mediation might be appropriate for your situation, and you're interested in the benefits of mediation, ask for a referral to a mediator. A good place to start is with referrals from mental health professionals, attorneys, clergy, or others who deal with mediators. Many national and state mediation associations provide useful information, as well as mediator referral services. Internet searching is another effective way to find a local mediator.

Remember, that divorce mediators come from a variety of backgrounds and, in addition to having extensive training and experience in mediation, will have expertise in such fields as mental health, law, business, and accounting, among others. A mediator should have experience and training that is appropriate to your particular situation. You should be comfortable with the mediator and feel that the mediator will be unbiased, open, helpful and capable of assisting you in negotiating your own decisions. A competent mediator should be able to explain and describe the legal requirements in your state for such issues as child support, parenting, equitable distribution, and spousal support. Interview more than one mediator and find one that you both are comfortable working with. Ask about relevant training, experience in handling situations similar to your case, and experience as a mediator and in other professions. Also, ask about fees, how long the process might take and about their resources for experts, as well as attorneys to assist with review of the Memorandum of Agreement.

Conclusion

There are many benefits to mediation. Mediation works because you make decisions together. You remain in control of the process, and you avoid the courtroom. The process includes just you, your spouse, and the mediator.

Mediation is today's alternative to a contentious divorce. Mediation is the better, easier, and less expensive way to get a divorce. Is it right for you?

Robert McDonnell, MS APM

Robert J. McDonnell, MS APM, owner and principal of Alliance Mediation Services, has been formally practicing mediation since 2003 and brings to his practice over thirty years of experience in the telecommunication industry, focused primarily on regulatory policy development and issue resolution.

He served as President – New Jersey Association of Professional Mediators (NJAPM), from October 2008 through September 2010. He currently serves on the NJAPM Board as Immediate Past President.

Robert is an Accredited Professional Mediator (APM) and received accreditation from the New Jersey Association of Professional Mediators. His practice includes both civil and family mediation services in New Jersey. He has also been accredited as an Advanced Mediator Practitioner by the Association of Conflict Resolution. Robert was trained in mediation and dispute resolution at Rutgers University, where he received a Graduate Certificate in Conflict Management. He holds a Masters of Science degree in Engineering Management and a Bachelor of Science in Electrical Engineering, and also attended graduate policy programs at Stanford and the University of Michigan.

Robert is approved by the New Jersey Administrative Office of the Courts (AOC) for the Presumptive Mediation Program for Civil, General Equity and Probate Cases and mediates civil cases for the AOC in several counties in Northern New Jersey. He is also on the New Jersey AOC Roster of Foreclosure Mediators. He volunteers his mediation services and serves as a mediator for the municipal courts in Essex, Morris and Passaic Counties.

He is also an arbitrator, and participates on the Financial Industry Regulatory Authority (FINRA) panels in New York and New Jersey.

Robert J. McDonnell, MS APM
Accredited Professional Mediator
Alliance Mediation Services
39 Alpine Drive
P.O. Box 87
Lincoln Park, NJ 07035-0087
Tel: 973 709-0188
Fax: 973 709-0255
rmcdonnell@alliance-mediation.com
www.alliance-mediation.com

SECTION 5

For Home Owners & Renters Alike: Preparing For and Surviving Natural Disasters & Financial Crisis

Financially Surviving Natural Disasters

by Terrence Coughlin, CPCU, ARM, AIC

Take steps to ensure your home owner's insurance claim is processed smoothly and quickly.

Nobody is ever really prepared when natural disaster strikes, however, the list below will help you be prepared in case of an emergency. A readiness plan will put you one step ahead of potential financial disaster:

BEFORE AN EMERGENCY

1) Verify that you have emergency phone numbers, including insurance and utility company numbers in more than one place, i.e. on your refrigerator, in your wallet, and programmed into your cell phone. Do not list any financial data that could compromise your account should it fall into the wrong hands!

2) Make sure that the electrical panel is properly labeled so that you can shut off electricity to specific parts of the home.

3) Know where your main utility shutoffs are located Gas, Oil, Water, etc! Learn how to shut them off and make sure whoever spends the most time at home knows this as well.

4) Have an evacuation plan for the house.

5) Make one of your New Year's resolutions to change the batteries in your smoke detectors on New Year's Day.

6) Think about getting a recordable smoke alarm. Some people believe that children are more likely to respond to the recording of a parent's voice telling them to get out of bed than to respond to the shrill sound of a smoke detector alarm.

7) Think about what can be grabbed on the way out before an event happens. Don't waste time during a crisis.

8) Scan insurance policies every year (this can be another New Year's resolution). Some policies are subject to subtle coverage changes. Scanning your policies will ensure that you have hard-copies when you need them. Scan a soft-copy to a disc or thumb-drive, or even cloud computing – scanning them to Google Docs or the like. Just make sure that a copy will survive if the house does not.

9) It is becoming more and more popular to scan important documents, photos and other paper belongings. There are many ways to back up these files offsite so that if the computer is destroyed, your valuable "memories" will still be recorded and available to you!

IN AN EMERGENCY

1) Ensure everyone is safely out.

2) Dial 911 once you are sure that your family and occupants are safe.

3) Turn off the utilities to your home.

4) Then you may then move your belongings or cover the belongings with tarps, if it is safe to do so.

AFTER THE EMERGENCY

- Call your insurance company's 24 hour claim line. Be careful of what you say. For example, if there is water in the basement, say exactly that. Do not say "Flood". Describe the condition and do not use general terms. Flooding is only if there is an inundation of surface water, instead of water running into the basement from a back up of sewer and drain.

- Be mindful of wording by saying "wind damage" or "storm damage", keep it simple. Wait until you have a clear picture of the damage before using descriptive wording.

- Be aware of the deductible issues in your policy. Many policies have a higher deductible for windstorm, a named storm or hurricane and tornados. Mislabeling the condition could cost you thousands. Be aware of exactly where the National Weather Service said there were tornadoes versus areas that just had heavy wind and rain.
- Know your policy before calling in the claim! When describing the damage, be specific to your policy. For example, there could be limitations for "silver" versus "collectibles".

Terrence Coughlin,

CPCU, ARM, AIC

Terrence P. Coughlin, CPCU, ARM, AIC is a professional Insurance and Risk Management Consultant with nearly thirty years of finance and insurance experience. He is the principle of Task Risk Management Consulting, Inc, located in Wyckoff, NJ. He has held senior positions in the finance and insurance brokerage arenas before spending the last ten years as a Risk Management Consultant.

In addition to his hands-on experience, Terrence has also worked hard on the technical/academic side; earning the Charter Property and Casualty Underwriter (CPCU) designation, which is the most advanced designation in the insurance industry. In addition to earning his CPCU, he has also earned his Associate in Risk Management (ARM) and Associate in Claims (AIC) Designations.

Terry Coughlin continues to keep up-to-date on his insurance knowledge by teaching CPCU and ARM courses on a regular basis. He is also a member of the Society of Risk Management Consultants (SRMC) and is a Past President of the New Jersey Chapter of the CPCU Society.

Task Risk Management Consulting, Inc.
Terrence P. Coughlin, President
CPCU, ARM, AIC
245 Braen Ave, Suite F
Wyckoff, NJ 07417
(201) 425.8363 Office
(201) 425.8398 Fax
coughlin@taskrmc.com email
taskrmc.com website

Mortgage Modification – Use It And Save Your Home & Your Sanity

by Vivian Gaspar & V. James Castiglia, Esq.

Foreclosure and Short Sale are terms that unfortunately have become all too common place recently. Often they are thought to be the only road to go down for those who have been affected by the economy because of a recent drop in income, a life change or are just unable to refinance due to the changes in the banking guidelines. A mortgage-modification is restructuring (making changes to) the terms of your existing mortgage. It is not a refinance, and there are no closing costs. There might however be minor fees which your lender may charge. The main way to be certain they are modifying your mortgage vs. refinancing is that modification fees will never include the recollecting of your property taxes for escrow.

Mortgage modification may get existing mortgages to an affordable rate and, some cases, get a relief period of between 2 to 5 years and a payment rate of between 2% to 4%. Also, forbearances are possible, which can vary from lender to lender. Ask your lender what they can offer. The average person has an interest rate of 6%. Imagine you would now pay half to a third of that payment to help them stay in their homes and prevent the ever increasing American ghost town.

The HAMP or Home Affordability Mortgage Protection Act which is also known as the "making home affordable" act was enacted in March 2009. The basic benefit is to bring the mortgage payment down to 31% mortgage debt to income ratio or an effective 2% mortgage interest rate for 60 months with the rate increasing by 1% a year until it is back to your current interest rate. There are several caveats to this program however, such as the loan amount cannot exceed $729,000 for a single family, the property must be owner occupied and that the home owner cannot be more than 12 months in arrears with payments. Also, it is very important that the borrower's monthly income needs to be in a very specific ratio of 3x the proposed modified payment including property taxes, homeowner's hazard insurance and any associated association dues. The reason is that if your gross household income is less than 3x that the idea is you cannot even afford a modified payment over time and if your income exceeds that 3x calculation than they deem you should be able to afford your mortgage payment. They also will take into account your net income and your expenses. However, there are some point of logic that will apply, such as: have you taken vacations or purchased non-necessity large ticket items when you fell behind in your mortgage payments or do you have multiple car payments and cannot pay your mortgage? (They will say get a used car without car payments so you can save on monthly expenses.) Also, small independent lenders can refuse to modify at all.

Mortgage Modification - Frequently Asked Questions

Question #1:

Is my credit score, current home value, or available equity factors for qualification?

Answer #1:

Short Answer: No.

Long Answer: While these are not factors for qualification, significant equity in a home may impact negotiation or qualification.

Question #2:

Who is a good candidate for a mortgage-modification?

Answer #2:

Any homeowner who is having a hardship. Good examples include:

a) Home-owners that have had an ARM reset higher; experienced a job loss or loss of 2nd income; experienced a divorce; caring for an elderly parent; experienced a sickness or incurred medical expenses; other hardship where loss of income or increased expenses have occurred.

b) Business-owners whose personal income has decreased as a result of a drop in business revenues.

Question #3:

Does a mortgage-modification effect my credit score?

Answer #3:

Yes, however to what degree is not an exact answer. Don't forget your credit score is comprised of several factors such as the number of credit accounts you have open and for how long, any judgments or liens, also ratio of available and used credit per credit card are just a few examples of how your total credit score is comprised and on what factors your credit history is judged.

Question #4:

What information is needed in order to have my mortgage modified?

Answer #4:

1. Information on your current mortgage, including: Principle Amount; Interest Rate; Mortgage Term; Monthly Payment (with & without escrows); Annual Taxes; Mortgage Lender; Loan Origination Date; Is Homeowners Insurance escrowed?; Explanation of hardship. Provide this information for each mortgage note.

2. Supporting documentation, including: Last years tax return; Last four pay-stubs or unemployment stubs; Last four bank statements; Current mortgage statement.

Question #5:

What are your recent success stories?

Answer #5:

See below - 13 recent successes in 2010:

<u>Case #1:</u>

Customer's monthly mortgage payment was reduced by 57% for a two year period. The money saved was completely forgiven by the bank, and not owed on the back end of the mortgage.

<u>Case #2:</u>

Customer's interest rate went from 10% to 3.9% for a five year period (they did not have to refinance). The money saved was completely forgiven by the bank, and not owed on the back end of the mortgage.

<u>Case #3:</u>

Customer did not pay the mortgage for two years and owed $52,000 in arrears to the bank (sheriff's sale was imminent). Our attorney stopped the sheriff's sale, and negotiated a 90% forgiveness of arrears, in addition to an affordable monthly payment.

Let's be more clear on this: In the end, the customer only had to pay $5,200.00 of the original $52,000.00, plus the negotiated affordable mortgage payment.

<u>Case #4:</u>

Customer's monthly mortgage payment went from $3,500 a month to $1,900 a month.

Case #5:

Customer's monthly mortgage payment went from $4,800 a month to $3,200 a month.

Case #6:

Customer's monthly mortgage payment went from $2,000 a month to $1,300 a month.

Case #7

Customer's monthly mortgage payment went from $6,188 a month to $2,828 a month.

Case #8:

Customer's monthly mortgage payment went from $3,600 a month to $2,117 a month.

Case #9:

For a second Mortgage:

Customer's monthly mortgage payment went from $611 a month to $298 a month.

Case #10:

Customer's monthly mortgage payment went from $4,055 a month to $2,943 a month.

Case #12:

Customer's monthly mortgage payment went from $2,548 a month to $1,700 a month during trial period then to $1,348 for permanent modification.

Case #13:

Second Mortgage: - Offer In Compromise:

$64,000 owed was negotiated to be completely settled for $15,000 cash lump sum. (Lump sum can be borrowed form any source of customer's choice.)

In some cases, principle balance reduction can be negotiated (as we have done) as a "reward" for making modified payments on time as much as $70,000 per year is possible.

Again, it is really important to realize that the "business" of mortgage modification is constantly changing and what the individual banks/lenders are willing to actually do to assist the homeowner is also ever changing. The federal government has stepped in, however their regulations set forth in the "making home affordable" guidelines have been followed to varying degrees by different lenders. The key is to be persistent and not take the first denial as the final word and to research the guidelines of your state's department of banking as to who is legally allowed to assist with mortgage modification if you choose to go that route. If you are going to do the modification effort without assistance then do your due diligence and carefully research the guidelines for the "making home affordable" modification program and make sure you follow the guidelines on how they want the information presented and be outspoken with working with your lender on what the guidelines state. Do not just settle for inferior in-house programs which are likely to have less of a reduction of payment for less time. Read the modification agreement very carefully before signing and if possible have it reviewed by an experienced real estate attorney. Remember, most modifications have trial payments that can not be late by even one day or they can deny you for the permanent, long-term modification. Also, equally important, you may constantly and continually be under scrutiny during the trial period until the final modification is signed by borrower and lender.

Understanding The Foreclosure Process – Why To Short Sale Vs. Foreclosure

by Vivian Gaspar & V. James Castiglia, Esq.

The housing crisis, which started in 2007, was attributed to many factors. The consequences included the closing of thousands of mortgage banks of all sizes, (among them the U.S.'s largest sub-prime lender, New Century which had closed over $50 Billion in mortgage loans just the prior year). Many experts have pointed the blame at the loose lending practices of the very banks which closed and fell victim to the domino effect of their own over-flexible lending guidelines. The bottom line is now what happens to the individual home owners who got caught up in this mortgage mess in one way or another?

Education is and should be the homeowner's primary tool in understanding not just their rights and obligations but their options as what to do and what not to do.

The first thing that a home owner should NOT do is give up too easily or move out of their home prematurely when they fall behind in payments. In the news there have been reports of homeowners putting the keys to their homes into envelopes and mailing them to their mortgage lender and moving out of the home. The media has coined the term "jingle envelopes" for this very action. In some cases the homeowner did this as an act of defiance or to make a statement. More troubling is the homeowner who genuinely believes that by mailing back the keys of their home to their mortgage bank they are released from their mortgage obligation. This is completely false! The only way to release the homeowner of any further obligation on the mortgage of that home is by 1) paying it off in full, 2) obtaining a signed short sale agreement from the Lender authorizing a short payoff or 3) having a foreclosure lawsuit finalized by the lender against the borrower.

A foreclosure is the type of judgment that is filed against a borrower by the lending mortgage bank due to lack of payments by the homeowner / borrower. The enforcement action is to take legal ownership of the home away from the homeowner and transfer it to the Lender. This happens with a sheriff's sale which comes at the end of the foreclosure process. The homeowner can be evicted from the property only after this process. This process does vary from state to state since this is a legal action on the state and not the federal level. In some states the home owner can be more than 24 months (two years) in arrears before getting to the point of a sheriff's sale, while in other states a sheriff's sale action can come in as little as 5 months of non-payment of the mortgage. It is very important that if you fall behind in your mortgage payment that you check with your county sheriff's department to see how long the process takes in your state. Also, it is important to understand what happens after the sheriff's sale. Does the home owner need to vacate the property the same day? In some cases, believe it or not, you can actually pay rent to the very lender which foreclosed upon you to actually continue to reside in the home (you once owned) as a paying tenant!

If you want to move on with your life and move out of the home (perhaps, the lender will not rent to you or you owe much more than the value of the home) you need to understand the differences and when and why to do a short – sale vs. allowing your home to be foreclosed upon. Following are the options to a foreclosure / sheriff's sale:

Traditional Sale – you sell your home with or without the aid of a realtor and you sell the home for more than you owe on the mortgage and are able to pay off the mortgage in full to the mortgage lender to whom you were paying the mortgage.

Short Sale – as the name implies – you sell your home and if your accepted purchase price is less than your mortgage balance (how much you owe on the original mortgage plus any arrears balance) you then need to negotiate (normally with the assistance of an attorney who specializes in this area) with your mortgage lender to accept the purchase price less any realtor and attorney fees (if applicable). This is to your advantage because then *your lender* had l*egally released you from any further debt and financial obligation* for *that property.* The Lender will take all of the proceeds of a short sale, the Sellers do not walk away with any money.

Foreclosure – when your home is foreclosed upon and the Sheriff's sale takes place many times the lender buys back the home from themselves then lists it for sale on the open market as "bank owned". Most or many times the bank sells the home at a loss to them. That means that they sell the home for less than was owed to them. It is possible that the lender can sue the homeowners who they foreclosed upon for the difference. As an example — Mr. & Mrs. Smith had their home sold at a sheriff's sale (foreclosure) and they owed $300,000. However, when the mortgage company they owed that mortgage balance to sold the house they were only able to sell it for $250,000 but they had to pay realtor fees and attorney fees totaling $20,000. Therefore, the mortgage lender will see that as a $70,000 loss to them and can potentially pursue Mr. & Mrs. Smith for that loss. Even if the mortgage lender says to the Smiths that they will forgive that loss the Smiths should verify if that lender will do so in a manner which will cause them to have a tax implication. That means that the lender will send them a 1099 for the forgiven amount which can be added to the Smith's income and can cause them to owe the IRS on that amount as if it were earned income. Because of this aspect you need to contact your tax professional before accepting any offers of forgiveness of debt by any debtors.

For the aforementioned reason, as well as other potential liability risks, selling your home either traditionally or through a short sale agreement is the more finalized and cleaner alternative to foreclosure.

Vivian Gaspar

As the Public Relations Director for an attorney specializing in mortgage modification, Vivian Gaspar has helped over 200 families to stay in their homes, and in some cases escape foreclosure all together. Ms. Gaspar had also been a recruiter, mortgage originator and a real estate agent. As a prior business owner she had been interviewed on television, newspaper and radio. Her business experience has helped her in advising her mortgage modification clients in their hardships.

Ms. Gaspar has been the founder and owner/operator of several businesses over the last 25 years. She has also been a public speaker on topics ranging from ID Theft to Mortgage Facts For Everyone. As someone who has worked individually with over 200 families in financial crisis in the last two years (as the Public Relations Director & Mortgage Modification Specialist in the legal office of V. James Castiglia in New Jersey) she heard similar stories and gave the same advice to people repeatedly. Her experience ranged from owning a marketing company to being a recruiter to being a mortgage loan officer which helped her in deciphering people's current mortgages as the first step in Mortgage Modification consultations. During the mortgage modification appointments she always started off by reviewing the client's origination documents to ensure that they had been fully aware of the specifics of their current mortgage. Unfortunately, Ms. Gaspar had found that over half of her modification clientele had been misled by the loan officer who placed those clients into the mortgage that currently needed modification.

Part of her responsibilities as Mr. Castiglia's Public Relations Director was to give speeches at civic organizations such as the Lions Clubs and Rotary Clubs. After several of these speeches, Ms. Gaspar had been approached with the suggestion to spread her knowledge to a wider audience and to consider writing a book. In February of 2010, she started giving the idea of writing a book on mortgage modification and the foreclosure process more serious consideration. Over the next few months Ms. Gaspar had concluded that she could help a wider base of people in crisis if she covered a broad subject base.

Ms. Gaspar started an outline of chapters on topics she wanted to see included in the book. Immediately she thought of all the business contacts she had accumulated over her years of attending business networking events, including those she organized and hosted. She was the founding member of the only lunch time Le Tip on the East Coast and founded her own location of Network Plus where the meetings were held every week for over a year. Ms. Gaspar had met several of the contributing authors at events which she hosted in 2009 and 2010 in Morris County, New Jersey. It was the knowledge of seasoned professionals that Ms. Gaspar wanted to bring to the general public. These topics had been created and outlined by Ms. Gaspar and included the expertise of 26 professionals in 38 chapters.

Ms. Gaspar's first book, "How to Survive Your Financial Crisis", is being released in February 2011 with the Spanish translation set to release in the Summer of 2012 along with a second edition as well as that edition's Spanish version to be released within 90 days thereafter.

Ms. Gaspar also envisioned the translation of both editions into the top 10 languages spoken throughout the world, with international sales and marketing through the website: www.howtosurviveyourfinancialcrisis.com.

V. James Castiglia, Esq.

Jim Castiglia graduated from Montclair Academy in 1970 and earned his Bachelor of Arts degree from Dickinson College, Carlisle, PA in 1974. He also had the privilege of studying for a year at the College's Center for European Studies at the University of Bologna, Italy. He earned his Doctor of Laws degree from Seton Hall University School of Law in 1977. He has been in private practice his entire career, first in West Orange, NJ and for the last 19 years in Oak Ridge, NJ (Morris Co.)

Jim's practice focuses on individual, family and small business legal needs. He is particularly experienced in residential and commercial real estate. He began doing loan modifications before the government's HAMP program was announced and has always processed loan modifications in-house. He helps people in foreclosure by representing them at foreclosure mediation hearings and uses the hearings as a means to obtain a loan modification. In the last several years a large part of his real estate practice has been mortgage modification negotiation, foreclosure prevention through mediation hearing as well as the quick disposition of short sales, both for the Buyer and the Seller.

He is active in his local Jefferson Township Rotary club and is active in the national leadership of his college fraternity, Alpha Chi Rho.

He has three college age children.

V. JAMES CASTIGLIA
A Professional Corporation
Counsellor at Law
5701 Berkshire Valley Road, Oak Ridge, NJ 07438
973-697-1676 • Fax 973-697-1053
vjc@vjamescastiglia.com

Reverse Mortgages
A Financial Option For Seniors

by Peter Nagy

What is a reverse mortgage? A reverse mortgage is a loan against your home that you do not have to pay back for as long as you live in your home. It can help turn the appraised market value of your home into cash without having to make monthly mortgage payments; and help better manage your financial future. Rather than making a monthly mortgage payment, you actually receive funds from the lender based on the loan terms that you select. Perhaps best of all, a reverse mortgage allows you to still own your home throughout the entire term of the loan.

Let your home take care of you: Reverse mortgages can be a great way for qualified homeowners who are 62 years of age or older to access the equity in their homes. A reverse mortgage can provide you with a source of funds to supplement your monthly income, cover healthcare costs, pay off existing mortgages or other financial obligations, fix up your home, or simply gain peace of mind. Whatever your specific goals, a reverse mortgage can go a long way towards helping you maintain your financial independence.

Benefits of a reverse mortgage:

-No monthly mortgage payments

- No income qualifications

- Loan proceeds may be tax-free-consult a tax advisor for more information

- The loan is not due until the last homeowner sells or permanently leaves the home

- Neither you nor your heirs will owe more than your home's appraised market value at the maturity of the loan

- You decide how you would like to receive the loan proceeds-lump sum, line of credit, monthly payments, or a combination of any of these.

Achieve your goal:

With a reverse mortgage, you have the freedom and flexibility to use the money from your home in any manner you see fit. Experience indicates that people use the funds for a variety of reasons including:

1. Healthcare and prescription drug costs
2. Home remodeling or repair
3. Supplemental income for everyday living expenses
4. Assisting grandchildren with educational expenses
5. Estate and financial planning
6. Long-term care insurance

Explore whether a reverse mortgage program would fit your needs

Assistance is available to explain your various reverse mortgage options and to help you determine if a reverse mortgage best addresses your financial needs. If you decide a reverse mortgage is the right solution for you, the next step is determining which reverse mortgage loan program works best for your particular situation.

Qualifying can be easy:

Although the qualification process may vary by lender, there are typically no income or health qualifications and only minimal credit score requirements needed to qualify for a reverse mortgage.

The amount of the reverse mortgage loan for which you qualify is determined by several factors, including:

1. Homeowner age-all homeowners must be at least age 62
2. Current appraisal value of your home
3. Current interest rate

Easy steps to getting a reverse mortgage:

The steps outlined below are intended to help you understand each stage of the loan process.

1. Get Educated

Regardless of the reverse mortgage program you choose, counseling by a Department of Housing and Urban Development (HUD)-approved counselor or a American Association of Retired Persons (AARP)-approved counselor is required. The counselor is there to help you make sure that you are fully aware of your options and that you understand the reverse mortgage program and the loan process itself.

With your consent, a representative of your lender may arrange for a HUD-approved counselor to contact you, or they may provide you with a list of approved counseling agencies in your area. In addition to counseling, you are encouraged to also seek advice from your family, legal, and financial advisors.

2. Appraisal

Upon completion and submission of your application, the lender will schedule an appraisal to determine the current market value of your home and whether or not any repairs will be needed in order to meet loan underwriting guidelines.

3. Underwriting

Underwriters will then review the loan file and appraisal in accordance with the applicable FHA or lender loan policy.

Upon completion, a representative of your lender will notify you of the lender's decision and inform you of any conditions that must be met prior to loan closing.

4. Loan Closing

If approved, you will then decide how you want to receive your cash from the loan proceeds. The final step will be signing the documents at loan closing. Disbursement of payment from your reverse mortgage loan may begin just days after closing.

5. Get started today

Call for more information and help in determining if a reverse mortgage best addresses your financial needs.

You've been taking care of your home for years. Isn't it time your home started taking care of you?

6. How much can be borrowed?

In most cases, maximum reverse mortgage loan amounts are based on the following factors:

- The age of the youngest homeowner
- The appraised value of your home
- The current interest rate
- The locally established lending limit

In general, the older you are, the more your home is worth, and the lower the interest rate, the more you will be able to borrow. Ask your reverse mortgage specialist for further details.

Peter Nagy
Reverse Mortgage Specialist

Peter is a reverse mortgage professional who truly enjoys working with seniors and changing their lives for the better.

The most successful reverse mortgage professionals treat the category as their main line of business, not a sideline. Peter is dedicated to stay abreast of the latest developments in the mortgage industry, which undergoes constant change in their guidelines and regulations. It takes a special kind of person to truly excel in the reverse mortgage business which involves educating prospective senior clients, and allowing them to take all the time they need to make a decision they're comfortable with.

Peter is a graduate of American University in Washington, DC where he obtained a Bachelors degree in marketing and finance. He is also a Certified Credit Consultant and speaks nationally to mortgage brokers/bankers, real estate agents and financial professionals about how to help their clients achieve the credit scores they truly deserve.

Peter states that, "I really enjoy the business of mortgage banking because I have the opportunity to consult my clients with regard to a major financial transaction in their life. Ultimately, they are grateful when I put them into a mortgage program that not only fits their needs but also their budget. As a trusted advisor, I take great pride in knowing that I am doing what's in the best interest of my clients."

Peter Nagy
Licensed Mortgage Originator
NMLM 207869
pnagy@kastlemortgage.com.
973-985-1680

SECTION 6

General Finance for Everyone

About My Mortgage

by Stephanie Banks

A woman said to me the other day, "UH! Refinance! I don't want to go through THAT again!"

Given the fact that rates are now at historic lows, and she stood to save a substantial amount on her monthly mortgage payment, I should have been shocked. However, I understood her pain. Whether a refinance or a new purchase, many of us have had long, agonizing, drawn out, mortgage experiences.

There are many reasons an otherwise smooth process becomes stressful, and those reasons lie on both sides of the fence. In the next few pages, I hope to shed some light on residential mortgages and the lending process, hopefully enabling you to make informed decisions in meeting your financing goals.

In The Beginning

When shopping for a mortgage, many of us start out by doing some research online, filling out short forms, looking for the best rates that will save us the most money. We may get calls from various mortgage companies, or we may venture out to our neighborhood lender.

No matter whom you do business with – a mortgage banker or a Mortgage Broker – you should only work with a Licensed Mortgage Professional.

Back in the early 2000's when home values were ridiculously off the charts, people were coming out of the wood work to become a Loan Officer and take advantage of you – I mean – the good living there was to be made. People with no prior financial or sales experience were working in this industry because borrowers were suddenly equity rich on paper. It didn't take a rocket scientist to convince that borrower to refinance their precious home and take cash out for other things (usually to pay off debt that was re-accumulated shortly afterward). To add insult to injury, more often than not, that well meaning borrower was put into a loan that they didn't qualify for, or should not have been in such as: Pay Option Arms for people who wanted to stay in their homes long term, No Documentation loans, No down payment or 100% financing for people whose credit was short of stellar. The result has been disastrous. Let me pause for a moment and make it clear that obviously not all mortgage people were licking their chops. The good ones then are the best ones now, professional, caring and responsible individuals who have built relationships with their clients. So why did all those nice borrowers (maybe you!) get swept up in the craziness? Well, because, you trusted us. And why shouldn't you? We are the experts in home financing. You wouldn't come to us with a sore throat, anymore than you would go to your doctor for your home loan. Unfortunately, the mortgage industry had their share of quacks as well, but unlike the medical and other professions, we were not required to be licensed, there was virtually no standard or regulation, and many a mortgage company turned a blind eye toward compliance laws because no one was looking over their shoulder.

Problem Solved

In July of 2008, the Office of the Comptroller of the Currency, Board of Governors of the Federal Reserve System, Federal Deposit Insurance Corporation, Office of Thrift Supervision, Farm Credit Administration, and National Credit Union Administration ("the agencies") published the final rules for implementing the federal registration requirements of the Secure and Fair Enforcement of Mortgage Licensing Act of 2008 (S.A.F.E. ACT), otherwise known as Public Law 110-289, Title V.

All mortgage banks, mortgage brokers and individual mortgage originators were required to be licensed by National Mortgage Licensing System and Registry in order to continue working in the industry. It requires 20 hours of educational courses, passing the federal licensing exam, extensive back round checks including fingerprinting on the federal and state level as well as proving financial responsibility. Additionally, each state that we originate loans in requires course work in that states mortgage and compliance laws and passing the state licensing exam.

So how do you know if the Loan Officer you are doing business with is licensed?

Licensed companies and individuals are given a unique identifying number. It is required to appear on all *business cards* and other forms of advertising. If you are doing business with someone who cannot provide a licensing number that is attached to THEIR name, not their companies name, you should probably turn on your heels and scoot. The National Mortgage Licensing System and Registry (NMLS) has a website www.nmlsconsummeraccess.com that has information on all licensed and registered individuals and companies nationwide. To be fair, when looking someone up by name, make sure to have their full name including middle initial or spelling out if necessary. Loan Officers who are employed by federally charters banks, savings and loan or credit unions do not have to be licensed, but are still registered as are their respective institutions, with the NMLS. You will find their names on the registry as well.

Mortgage Banker vs. Broker vs. Your Hometown Bank

Now that you're ready to find that perfect mortgage, what type of mortgage professional will best suit your needs?

Mortgage banks are state licensed, originate loans directly to the borrower, and fund loans using their *own capi-*

tal. The advantages to working with a mortgage banker are many. In addition to offering competitive rates, they basically have control of the total lending environment. In other words, origination, processing and underwriting are done "in house", allowing for a more personal touch to your particular scenario. The communication between all parties involved has virtually 0 degrees of separation, resulting in an efficient and quick delivery of the loan approval and clear to close.

Mortgage bankers lend their own product line, which some may see as a limiting disadvantage. However, many mortgage bankers have a varied product line and are highly competitive in the market. Costs should be lower when working with a mortgage banker as well because there are no "middleman" fees.

A Mortgage Broker is an intermediary who puts the borrower together with the lender (mortgage banker). Their product line can be as varied as the lenders they do business with, enabling them to accommodate many lending needs. However, as the middle person they are working with processors and underwriters who are employees of the various lenders, not their co-workers. Although this works, those same processors, underwriters and closers are also working on files from their in house loan officers. Your file is from the broker who is calling in.

Additionally, Mortgage Brokers cannot lock your rate or grant you a pre-approval. All decisions come directly from the lender they are submitting your application to. By the nature of the process, closing times can be extensive as well, - between 30- 60 days.

Your Neighborhood Savings and Loan may already have a relationship with you if you are an account holder, although it's not a prerequisite for a loan. However, this is not their primary business and their mortgage products may not be as competitive. In most instances, even with the large household name banks, your application is taken at the branch level by a customer service representative. With all respect due to them, they are not usually privy to lending guidelines. You application is then submitted to a corporate mortgage department and out of the hands of the original person who took your information. Lending guidelines can be stricter as well, so unless you are the perfect borrower, don't expect to be offered a chair and a cup of coffee much less a mortgage.

The Best of Both Worlds is the mortgage banker who has an extensive product line AND can broker out any special situations that his/her product guidelines don't normally accommodate.

What's Your Rate?

My intention was to segue into "Types of Mortgages" at this point in the chapter, but since this is the question everyone asks first, it pulled rank. First of all, when it comes to buying a home or refinancing, you can no longer shop for a mortgage based simply on lowest interest rate quotes. Today's consumer needs good advice from an experienced, educated mortgage professional who has the consumer's best interest in mind.

This means BEWARE of anyone who quotes you an interest rate over the phone or the Internet without asking anything about you, your family, your finances or your lifestyle. Besides market conditions, your mortgage rate is based on a long list of criteria that are unique to your individual financial situation.

Look at the list below of *15 different criteria* that affect your *mortgage rate*. How can anyone quote you an interest rate you can trust without a thorough knowledge of your unique financial situation?

1. Amount of Mortgage
2. LTV (loan to value ratio) based on value of your property
3. Type of Property - primary residence, investment, do you collect rent, is it a PUD or condo, do you pay association fees
4. DTI (debt to income ratio)
5. Type of Employment and Income (are you a W-2 employee, 1099, or self employed, are you retired, collecting SS and a pension, early retirement with just a pension. Are you on disability –permanent or temporary, are you on family leave, returning to the same job, are you a union worker with sporadic employment, are you on temporary layoff?)
6. Type of Loan
7. Cash- out or a rate and term refinance
8. Do you escrow your taxes and insurance
9. What is your credit score?
10. If a purchase – how much of a down payment do you have?
11. Is any of your down payment a gift
12. What kind of assets do you have and can you document them
13. Length of Loan
14. Co–borrower (all of the above)
15. Will you pay Points

What Causes Interest Rate Movement

The Federal Reserve constantly evaluates the US economy and, when necessary, takes steps to address inflationary concerns and avoid economic recession or depression. The mass media, in turn, reacts by providing a wide range of opinions and interpretations of the Fed's monetary policy. This can make it very difficult for consumers to decipher how such actions will influence interest rates in general and mortgages in particular.

And although actions of the Federal Reserve can have a direct impact on the Prime rate, mortgage interest rates are dictated by the trading of mortgage-backed securities, which are similar to bonds and trade on a daily basis. This means that the real dynamic at the heart of interest rate movement is the competitive relationship between stocks and bonds.

Stocks, bonds, and mortgage-backed securities compete for the same investment dollars on a daily basis. There is literally only so much money to be invested. When the Federal Reserve feels that interest rates need to be decreased in an effort to stimulate the economy, this reduction in rates can often cause a stock market rally. When the market becomes bullish, the money to invest in stocks comes from the selling off of other investments, including mortgage-backed securities.

Unfortunately, when mortgage-backed securities are sold off to fuel stock market rallies, this causes interest rates to go up, not down.

Historically, there have been many instances where the Federal Reserve has increased interest rates, arousing fears that corporate profit margins would be affected. This resulted in stocks being sold off, leading money managers to search for a place to invest their newly liquidated assets until the next market rally. One such safe haven has been mortgage-backed securities, which cause mortgage rates to drop.

The daily ebb and flow of money is what matters most when it comes to the movement of mortgage interest rates. I make it a point to continuously monitor interest rates for my clients and advise them of opportunities to manage their mortgage debt at a better rate. This is the foundation of my business model as a trusted advisor.

What type of mortgage is best for me?

Finding a mortgage that's right for you should be easy. However, there are often many different programs to choose from, as well as a myriad of ways to structure your loan in terms of the amount financed, term, payment, rate, closing costs and so forth.

Because there are so many options available, it's important to seek advice from an experienced mortgage professional who is looking out for your interests. The first step in determining which program is right for you is to ask yourself the important questions listed below. These questions can also help you confirm that you've chosen the right mortgage professional as well, because he or she should be asking you the same questions before trying to put any mortgage in place:

- How long do you anticipate living in your home?
- Do you expect any changes over the next few years, such as expanding your family or having children go off to college or even move away?
- Do you expect any changes in income such as promotions, downsizing, retirement, inheritance, or pensions?
- Are you expecting a change with regard to your investments?
- When it comes to investment strategies, are you conservative, aggressive, or somewhere in between?

These questions are important in that different loan programs will offer specific benefits that will appeal to borrowers at different stages of life. What one homeowner might find desirable might cause another to reach for the antacids!

Your mortgage professional should give you a complete picture of exactly how much your mortgage will cost over the period of time you anticipate having the loan. This is the single most important factor you should consider when shopping for a mortgage. Not only does this data illustrate the bigger picture of your financial goals, it allows for adjustments should things change a little sooner than expected. A good timeframe for this projection is anywhere from three, five, or even up to seven years.

Types of Mortgages

Whether a refinance or a new purchase, there are many types of mortgage products to choose from, each having advantages and disadvantages depending on your situation. Because this is the largest investment most people make, it is important that you do some research and gain some understanding as to what is best for you. Your mortgage professional, in my opinion is OBLIGATED to educated you and make sure you understand the mortgage product they are qualifying you for and why. Don't forget the old adage, "there is no such thing as a stupid question." Ask, ask, ask, until you are comfortable.

Fixed Rate Mortgages

30 year Fixed Rate Mortgages - This is the one most folks are looking for. It is also the mortgage product that makes the most sense if you plan to own you home for more than 5 years. The advantages are the obvious protection against inflation – if rates go up, yours won't. You always know what your interest is going to be, regardless of what's happening in the market, making it a low risk mortgage. Additionally, it allows you to budget and plan for other long term financial goals because you know what your payment will be for the life of the loan.

Other factors to consider with a fixed rate mortgage is that even though the rate stays the same, if your taxes or homeowners insurance increase, obviously so will your payment. Also, if mortgage rates go down, the only way to take advantage of a lower payment would be to refinance. The most important factor, however, is that 30 year fixed rates are traditionally higher than other loans products such as adjustable rate mortgages. Therefore you may not be able to qualify for as large a loan amount.

Fixed rate mortgages are available as 40, 30, 25, 20, 15 and 10 year loans. It is important to understand that even thought the rates may be lower on a shorter term mortgage, the payment is usually higher because you are financing over a shorter period of time. This may sound pretty obvious, but you would be surprised how many people tell me they are looking for a lower rate, lower payments AND to shorten the term of the mortgage. Not usually happening. As an example:

The payment on a $200,000 mortgage at 5.00% for 30 years would be $1073.64

The payment on a $200,000 mortgage at 4.50% for 15 years would be $1529.99

In order for the 15 year payment to be lower than the borrowers current 30, he would have to currently be paying a rate of 8.5% or higher.

A quick word about 40 year loans - yes, the payments are lower, enabling you to qualify for a larger loan. After all, you are spreading those payments out over an extra 10 years. However, not only is the interest rate usually a bit higher, you are also paying that interest over an additional 10 years, and paying toward principle at a much slower pace. Many lenders who offer this product amortize over a full 40 years - just like a 30 year mortgage, but 10 years longer. However, some 40 year products have a balloon payment at the end of 30 years

Hybrid Adjustable - (sometimes referred to as Short-Term Fixed Rate mortgages, or Hybrids) come in numerous varieties; the 3, 5, 7 and 10-Year Fixed. These are all 30-year loans that carry a fixed rate for a set number of years, and then roll over to an Adjustable Rate Mortgage.

For example, in a 7-Year Fixed Rate scenario, the rate would be fixed the first seven years, and the loan becomes an Adjustable for the remaining 23 years. The main advantage of these hybrid programs over a traditional 30-Year Fixed loan is typically a slightly lower interest rate.

These types of loans often work well for people who do not plan on being in their home for an extended period of time, such as first time home buyers. The most important question to ask when going into an Intermediate Fixed Mortgage is how long will the borrower need the money?

If the borrower intends to sell the home in four to five years, then a 5-Year Fixed loan offers stability and a lower interest rate for the time that money is needed. However, in this example it may not be wise to pay points up front to obtain a lower interest rate, because the likelihood of recuperating the cost of those points would be diminished because of the short time in the loan.

Please be aware that these are Adjustable Mortgages. I recently spoke to a gentleman who was working with another lender. He insisted that he was getting a 5 year fixed mortgage. The problem here was that it was presented to him by the loan officer in such a way that he believed his loan to be a kin to a 30 year traditional fixed rate loan. He had no idea it was an adjustable mortgage, and never would have agreed to that type of financing. He was told that after 5 years the rate would go up. He assumed that it would then stay at the new rate. It really didn't matter to him because he was convinced that he would be out of the house in five years anyway. However, the issue here is that he really didn't know the product. What if something in his life changed that prevented him from selling his home in 5 years, the rate started to adjust up (it can go down) and he was unable to refinance? Overall, this may have been the right product for his situation, but it wasn't presented to him truthfully and therefore prevented him from making an informed decision.

How Adjustable Rate Mortgages Work

During the last decade, Adjustable Rate Mortgages (ARMs) have increased in popularity among consumers. According to national studies, few homeowners (especially first-time buyers) remain in their homes for more than seven years. In this case, it often makes sense to get an adjustable rate mortgage with a lower rate, especially one with a 5-year or 7-year fixed portion, since they won't have the loan long enough to be concerned about rate fluctuation.

Adjustable Rate Mortgages have three main features: Margin, Index, and Caps. The Margin is the fixed portion of the adjustable rate. It remains the same for the duration of the loan. The Index is the variable portion. This is what makes an ARM adjustable. Margin + Index = Interest Rate.

It's important to understand that there are many different indices: The 11th District Cost of Funds (COFI), the Monthly Treasury Average (MTA), The One Year Treasury Bill, the Six Month Libor, etc. Each index has its own strengths and weaknesses; some are slow moving others are more aggressive.

The third and final component of Adjustable Rate Mortgages is Caps. Caps limit how much the rate can fluctuate over time. Annual Caps limit changes to the annual rate, whereas Life Caps provide a worst case scenario over the life of the loan.

FHA Loans - differ from typical loans in that they are insured by the Federal Housing Administration, which is a part of the Department of Housing and Urban Development (HUD). Because this insurance reduces the lender's risk on the loan, lenders have greater flexibility with regard to approving loans. For example, FHA loans are not as restrictive with minimum credit scores so a client may be able to obtain a loan despite having had credit problems or even a bankruptcy in the past. Alternatively, if a consumer does not have a significant traditional credit history, it may still be possible to obtain financing by documenting payment histories on items such as rent and utilities. Individual policies by lender may vary so ask your mortgage consultant for additional clarification.

FHA loans also provide added flexibility when it comes to closing costs and the down payment. Many of the closing costs can be incorporated into the loan, and a down payment of as little as 3.5% of the purchase price is required. The down payment may be obtained as a gift from a family member or through a down-payment assistance program. FHA loans are processed just like any other loan, and they provide a wonderful opportunity for consumers who are seeking to achieve home ownership!

The Advantages of FHA Loans

In many regions of the US, FHA loans have only recently come back into vogue, so a lot of real estate agents and mortgage originators aren't familiar with this great resource. The following are a just a few of the recent changes that have made FHA loans a more attractive option again for some consumers looking to buy a new home or refinance an existing one:

1) Congress passed the Stimulus Act of 2008. During the recent housing boom, home values surpassed FHA loan limits in many regions of the US. The recent enactment of this important legislation, however, increased FHA loan limits up to $729,500 in many high-cost regions of the US through the end of the year. FHA loan limits vary by county, so give us a call for loan limits in your area.

2) The FHA changed its appraisal and fee negotiating guide-

lines. In the past, many sellers steered clear of FHA loans because the appraisals were too strict and certain fees were non-negotiable. The FHA has greatly loosened these guidelines to make it easier for both buyers and sellers.

3) FHA loans are much cheaper now. Because FHA loans are federally insured, they tend to trade at a higher premium in the secondary market. This means lenders can often charge a lower rate.

4) FHA loans are typically not as credit-score restrictive. Borrowers usually can have a lower score than with other products and still qualify for a good rate.

5) FHA loans require as little as 3.5% down, and allow a) Sellers to contribute up to 6% of the buyer's purchase price to close; b) Homeowners to take cash out up to 85% of the home's value; and c) Homeowners to consolidate first and seasoned second mortgages up to 97.75% of the home's value.

A Word About Points and When Should You Pay Them

Points are up-front fees paid by the borrower to obtain a better interest rate on a loan. One point equals one percent of the loan amount. While a lower interest rate may result in a lower monthly payment, it is important to consider how long you intend to be in the loan and to compare current interest rates to historical market trends. This will help you to determine whether paying points is a worthwhile investment.

As an example - If you take out a $300,000 mortgage and decide to pay one point in order to lower your interest rate, this would translate into an up-front cost of $3,000. Just to keep it simple, we'll assume that paying this one point will save you $50 a month. This means it will take you 60 months to recoup the cost of that point. If you decide to refinance or sell the home before the 60-month mark, your money is lost –

not to mention the opportunity cost of not having this money invested elsewhere. In this scenario, you would only benefit financially from paying points if you were to remain in the home for no less than 60 months.

It's also important to remember that interest rates run in cycles. When rates are at historical lows, it makes more sense to pay points if you plan to live in the home for an extended period of time. If it's unlikely that rates will go down in the near future, then there will be no need to refinance.

When interest rates are high, however, there is a strong likelihood that they will come down again before too long. Therefore, this is not a good time to pay points. The chances of refinancing in the near future are extremely high, and you will likely not be in the loan long enough to recoup the up-front cost of the points.

Tax deductibility is another thing to consider when choosing whether or not to pay points. For new purchases, interest from both points paid and your mortgage are tax deductible up front. For refinances, however, points are not deductible up front. Instead the deductions are spread out over the term of the loan (unless the entire loan is paid off early), making points more costly in comparison.

Credit Scoring

There are five factors that comprise the credit score. They are listed below in order of importance, just as an underwriter would look at the score:

- Payment History: 35% impact. Paying debt on time and in full has a positive impact. Late payments, judgments and charge-offs have a negative impact. Missing a high payment has a more severe impact than missing a low payment. Delinquencies that have occurred in the last two years carry more weight than older items.

- Outstanding Credit Balances: 30% impact. This factor marks the ratio between the outstanding balance and available credit. Ideally, the consumer should make an effort to keep balances as close to zero as possible, and definitely below 30% of the available credit limit when trying to purchase a home.
- Credit History: 15% impact. This marks the length of time since a particular credit line was established. A seasoned borrower is stronger in this area.
- Type of Credit: 10% impact. A mix of auto loans, credit cards, and mortgages is more positive than a concentration of debt from credit cards only.
- Inquiries: 10% impact. This quantifies the number of inquiries that have been made on a consumer's credit history within a six-month period. Each hard inquiry can cost from 2 to 50 points on a credit score, but the maximum number of inquiries that will reduce the score is 10. In other words, 11 or more inquiries in a six-month period will have no further impact on the borrower's credit score.

Remember, a computer that's not taking any personal factors into consideration calculates these scores. When a credit report is generated, it is simply today's snapshot of your credit profile. This can fluctuate dramatically within the course of a week, depending on your activities. You should be aware that when you enter into the loan process, know that it's not in your best interest to go out on a shopping spree. Please make sure you are not creating a negative impact on your score while your lender is reviewing your file.

When a lender runs your credit, they are compiling a tri-merge credit report. This provides scores from the three credit bureaus, Experian®, TransUnion®, and Equifax. The lender should be provided with this rounded profile because these three scoring systems can vary in their results. The lender is going to look at the middle score and throw out the other two. In many cases, this works to the borrower's advantage.

What Constitutes Closing Costs?

Second to the popular question, "what are your rates?" is "what are your closing costs?" Closing costs are expenses that cover fees associated with the transfer of property ownership, fees paid to state and local governments, and the costs of obtaining a mortgage loan. In the case of a new purchase, some of these fees are negotiable, and could be paid by either the buyer or the seller. In all lending situations some costs are one-time fees (non-recurring closing costs, such as title search, termite inspection, appraisal, etc.); while other fees such as homeowner's insurance or property taxes are things you will expect to continue to pay on a regular basis as a homeowner.

When looking at closing costs, especially in the case of a refinance, usually the largest portion of money is appropriated for escrows, with the exception of points if you are paying them. If the lender is disclosing properly, these numbers should be relatively the same no matter who you are doing business with. Many times a lender will disclose 6 months taxes and insurance on the initial Good Faith Estimate, knowing that on the final Settlement Statement the number may be reduced to 3 or 4 months. Conventional wisdom says it's better to over disclose and have your numbers come down in the end as opposed to under disclosing. Unfortunately, many loan originators will under disclose because they are keenly aware of most borrowers apprehension of closing costs. As an example, they will disclose 2 months taxes and 2 months home owners insurance to be held in escrow. Another "trick" is the per diem interest. This interest is calculated based on your new rate and the day of the month you close. Many loan officers will calculate at one day as opposed to say 15 days. These two examples will heavily impact the bottom line. It will make their closing cost appear very low and cause the borrower to stop talking to anyone who is higher. Obviously, when the borrower gets to the closing table, they are in for a big surprise.

As part of the loan selection process, your mortgage consultant should be giving you some idea of how much money you should have in reserve to cover your end of these costs if you are not rolling it into the mortgage. The Real Estate Settlement Procedures Act (RESPA) requires the lender to provide you with a Good Faith Estimate within three days of the submission of your loan application.

RESPA also states that as a home buyer, you have the legal right to request a copy of the HUD-1 Settlement Statement 24 hours before your closing is scheduled. The HUD-1 clearly defines all closing costs, including those that are to be paid by the buyer and the seller. It's a good idea to have both of these forms before your closing so you can compare the estimated costs to the actual costs before you finalize your transaction.

Five Reasons to Refinance Your Mortgage

There is an old adage in the mortgage business that states that if you can improve your interest rate by at least two percentage points, then it is a good time to refinance. While that may work as a general rule of thumb, the truth is that there are many reasons to refinance. Here are a few:

Lower your interest rate.

Securing a lower interest rate is one of the top reasons for refinancing. This can make a big difference in your monthly out-of-pocket costs for housing and save money on financing fees.

Build equity faster.

If you are in a position to make higher monthly payments due to an increase in salary or other good fortune, you may want to switch from a 30-year loan program into a 15- or 20-year loan structure. This enables you to build equity faster and save a tremendous amount of money on financing fees.

Change your loan program.

Some homeowners who start out in an Adjustable Rate Mortgage (ARM) find that they would like to switch to the stability of a Fixed Rate mortgage at some point. An ARM may have been the most attractive rate and loan package when you first financed your home, but we can provide you with loan comparison charts to find out if you can save money with another type of loan program that might work better for you right now.

Credit score has improved.

If your credit score has improved as a result of making your mortgage payments on time and in full, you may be in a position to take advantage of your improved credit standing. We can review your current credit score, the terms of your existing mortgage, and review options for other loan programs that could not only reduce your monthly payment, but also save you money on interest fees paid over the life of the loan.

Use the equity you have established.

A cash-out refinance allows you to tap into the equity you have built up in your home. You may want to pay off revolving credit card accounts, send a child to college, or use the money for home improvements or personal expenses.

When shopping for a mortgage, you should always evaluate your choices carefully and consider how they will fit in with your long-term financial plan.

Stephanie M. Banks

Mortgagc Banker NMLS# 324908

When she was in the eighth grade, Stephanie's father bought her 20 shares of a mutual fund and a copy of the Wall Street Journal, handed it to her and said, "Now you're an investor, start learning". Fast forward 8 years - the Biology major who hung out at the Met, ended up with a series 6 NASD license selling mutual funds to business owners in SoHo.

After a few years working for a Wall Street Firm, Stephanie took her much desired Series 6 license and settled back in NJ at Equitable Insurance, licensed in Life, Accident and Health insurance. Ever the artist, a few years later she left the financial world to pursue a career in the restaurant industry, working her way up and eventually graduating from the Culinary Institute of America where she was awarded a graduate fellowship. After many successful years as Executive Chef for corporate clients, Stephanie realized the dream of homeownership and the potential hazards of placing your trust and hard earned money in the hands of lenders who may not have your best interests at heart. Stephanie's financial interest was rekindled as she learned about the mortgage industry and witnessed the unscrupulous behavior of many loan originators. She has been a mortgage consultant for 6 years, and has worked for both mortgage brokers and bankers. She entered the industry when in was common place to receive daily emails announcing the beginning of the end for many lenders.

Her passion is client education. She feels that in order for there to be a successful, long term client - trusted advisor relationship both loan officer and client education is necessary. "There are too many people that have mortgages whose only purpose was to line the pockets of uncaring, bad loan officers. People need to have faith and trust in the lending system again".

Stephanie lives in Southern New Jersey with her husband and daughter and their two dogs. She spent 6 active years as a leader in the Girl Scouts and is a member of her church choir. She is also a musician in piano, organ and voice in area churches.

Stephanie M. Banks
Mortgage Banker
Office 856-310-1300
Cell 732-486-5647

Bankruptcy – Understand The Basics

by Santo Bonanno, Esq.

Due to the economic crisis since 2007 – bankruptcy filings have doubled. Approximately 98% are individual filings vs. corporate. For the first time many other attorneys are sending clients to bankruptcy attorneys. The bankruptcy laws in NJ changed in 2005 and the requirement for attorney's due diligence for their liability. This change took place because large credit card companies have complained to congress then congress made changes such as requiring individuals to take credit counseling course. The course must take place before filing and a financial management course must be taken to marinating the discharge. This is a new federal law.

Bankruptcy is a federal law and someone has the right to elect if it benefits them. As one more extreme case, Florida has a homestead exemption state law which means the debtor (individual) can choose to keep the home regardless of the amount of debt as long as their mortgage is paid.

Bankruptcy is fairly universal in the laws and exemptions throughout the US. The most common causes for filling have been 1) loss of job 2) divorce 3) disability. The formula is if a person's debt is greater than $20,000; if the debt is less than settlement is sought. The reason for the $20,000 guideline is that it is federal law that each debtor is allowed to keep $15,000 of assets from creditors for their fresh start. The general cost for filling bankruptcy is $2,000 for chapter 7 & $3,000 for chapter 13.

The types of bankruptcy available for individuals are:

Chapter 7, Chapter 13 & Chapter 11: All 50 states require the attorney to disclose their fees on the petition anything that is beyond the initial retainer must be approved by a bankruptcy judge.

All trustees are attorneys who are full time attorneys but part time trustees who receive a flat fee for each case they handle pay to them by the US trustees' office.

The most common type of bankruptcy is Chapter 7 which is commonly called straight liquidation. It is used by individuals who have less than $20,000 in assets. In NJ, the exempt assets are: 401k, IRA and pensions, as an example. Therefore, the $20,000 in assets can be above and beyond the fore mentioned exempt assets.

Chapter 13 filings are for those who have more than $20,000 in assets and wish to protect them. This is done by giving the creditors between 5%-100% repayment plans based upon ability to repay which is not to exceed 60 months. The payments are done through a bankruptcy trustee who in turn pays the creditors at a 10% commission, which the trust gets for their service. The Chapter 13 trustee is appointed in each jurisdiction by the US trustee office. Jurisdictions are based on populations with no less than one per state.

Chapter 11 is for those individuals whose assets or liabilities exceed $650,000. Liabilities are the creditors. It operates the same as Chapter 13 however instead of paying a trustee you pay directly to your creditors. The cost of filing a chapter 11 is a minimum of $1,050 + attorneys retainer starts at $5,000.

For business owners can only file Chapter 7 or 11 if it is a corporation. Chapter 13 filing is only for individuals who have less than $650,000 of debts and assets.

How does a business owner close a business where they have signed personal guarantees? They must first do a business Chapter 7 for both their corporation and for themselves personally if they have signed any personal guarantees for corporate debit such as in the most common cases, corporate credit cards or leases or corporate lines of credit.

In a Chapter 7 filing of bankruptcy:

The trustee will do a liquidation analysis on all real estate owned by the debtor. This is usually just for the primary residence. The trustee will get an appraisal which is paid for by the debtor then 10% is subtracted for closing costs which covers real estate commission and transfer tax and also subtracts all mortgages against the property and lastly the Federal personal real estate exception of $20,400. If there is no equity left after that analysis then the trustee will abandon the property and you may keep your home as long as the debtor works out an acceptable mortgage modification with the mortgage holder.

If there is equity above the liquidation analysis, and you wish to retain the property, you can negotiate with the chapter 7 trustee to buy out the equity or a portion of the equity so that trustee will abandon the property.

~ What many be a surprise to many is what may be included in dischargeable debt: mechanics liens and judgments as well as 1040 IRS debt over 3 yrs old as long as neither were deemed to be was not fraud. ~

In a Chapter 13 filing of Bankruptcy:

As long as the debtor makes the payments into the approved plan to the chapter 13 trustee the home cannot be foreclosed upon. This type of bankruptcy stops any foreclosure process as long as the plan is approved and complied with.

Mortgage modification *can* be used with any type of bankruptcy at any state stage prior to sheriff sale which is the enforcement action of a foreclosure.

How does bankruptcy affect divorces? Bankruptcy does not eliminate child support, alimony, or any other provision of a support order that is entered by the matrimonial court.

Non bankruptcy debts are as follows:

- Sales and use taxes
- Federal withholding taxes if you are an employer
- Income taxes that are less than 3 years old and the returns have been filed
- Domestic support orders
- Injuries caused by drunk driving
- Any debt which was caused by fraud or mis-representation
- Criminal fines and restitution

Santo J. Bonanno, Esq.

Mr. Bonanno was born in New Jersey, completed 9 years of military academy education.

He graduated from the University of Bridgeport School of Law in 1980 receiving his Juris Doctor, and was admitted to the Connecticut Bar Association that same year. He was admitted to the New Jersey Bar Association in 1981. In 1989 he was admitted to the New York Bar Association.

BANKRUPTCY PRACTICE

Creditors' rights and bankruptcy related litigation

Chapter 7, liquidation cases

Chapter 11 and Chapter 13 reorganization cases

Mr. Bonanno has a wealth of experience in variety of civil actions in both federal and state courts as well as corporate and auditing experience, including a successful defense of prevailing wage before the NJ Supreme Court.

His education, B.S. in Accounting and M.S. in Taxation, and his work experience prior to going into private practice are most beneficial when handling corporate, commercial and bankruptcy matters. Mr. Bonanno worked as an IRS auditor and as an auditor for the State of Connecticut. Additionally, he was employed as a tax accountant for Richardson Merrill, (a pharmaceutical company) and a tax manager and corporate counsel for Lonza, Inc. (a chemical company). While residing in Franklin Lakes, NJ, for eighteen years, for thirteen years he served as a member of the Board of Education, including two terms as President of the Board. Additionally, he served on the Blue Ribbon Mayor's council committee and coached soccer for the Recreation Commission.

SANTO J. BONANNO, Esq.,
Attorney and Counselor at Law
1430 Route 23 North Wayne, NJ 07470
Tel: (973) 686-9060 Fax: (973) 686-9062
santobonanno@optonline.net

Save On Your Energy Bills

by Michael Menihan

Did you know that Electric and Natural Gas service are no longer monopolies in many states, and due to government deregulation, you have a choice of who generates your Electric and Natural Gas supplies?

Maybe you do know because you have been getting annoying sales calls telling you to switch, but you might think it's a scam. Well, I am here to tell you that it's not and you can save hundreds and maybe thousands of dollars a year depending on how much energy you consume in your home and/or small business.

The Power to Choose

Thanks to a national energy deregulation bill passed in 1999, residential and small business customers, in a number of states, can now manage and control their energy costs in ways never before thought possible.

Before deregulation you had no choice. You did not need to pay attention to the energy markets and you simply paid your bill like everyone else. But today you have the power to choose your supplier! The savings will not come to you by default; you must actively make a choice. In a deregulated market you must decide who to buy from, whether you should consider a market based (variable) rate or a (fixed) rate, where available. If you do not choose a new supplier the local utility by default will remain the supplier of your energy at the highest market rate permitted.

Electric - What was deregulated?

Simply put the supply portion of your electric bill, which is roughly 70% of the cost, was deregulated. The utilities sold off their power plants that generated the electricity, and now only own the transmission and distribution wires. They also serve as a 'default' for the supply to customers who do not shop for alternative electricity suppliers. With the move to competition, the utilities have separated their service into two parts:

- Regulated Distribution of Power (the Delivery), which is still only provided by the utility, and
- Supply, Bulk Generation Service (BGS), of the electric commodity is now open to competition.

Residential and Small Business customers (usually businesses consuming less than 10,000 kWh per month) who choose an alternate energy provider still have their power delivered, serviced, maintained and billed, to them, by their existing local utility. So the consumer doesn't experience any change in their electricity use, the only change will be the indication of the name of the alternative energy provider on the supply entry of their bill from the current utility provider.

Natural Gas - What was deregulated?

This works much like what was explained above. Likewise this bill has two components and the supply portion is the one where you can choose a new energy provider.

Types of Programs

If you have not chosen an alternate supplier you are paying a month-to-month variable rate based on filed tariffs for each service area. This is usually the most expensive rate that you can have since it is based upon the demand of the month in which you were billed. Like everything else in life, if you wait until the last minute to buy it you usually pay more. If you choose a new supplier you have the option of remaining on a month-to-month variable rate or choosing to lock in today's low rates for up to a year and sometimes longer. Energy costs are at or near their all-time lows so it makes sense to lock in for as long as you can to hedge rising energy costs and inflation.

Types of Sales People

You might be contacted by a direct sales person for one supplier, a broker that represents multiple suppliers, a direct mail flyer urging you to call a number to switch energy suppliers or you might hear a media (radio or TV) commercial. The sales person you deal with is paid a commission from the energy supplier, as you pay your monthly bill, so there should be zero cost to you the customer.

How does it work?

Your salesperson might take your information over the phone, or ask you to input your billing information on their website or have you fill out an enrollment form. So when you are ready to choose a supplier have your most recent energy bill in hand and ensure that you enter your information exactly as it appears on your current bill. If the information doesn't match your current bill exactly, your request could be rejected by your current utility/service provider.

If you decide to start saving by choosing a new supplier, there should be no cost to switch. You get the same electricity or natural gas from the same delivery company (utility), using the same poles, same wires, same gas mains and the same meters. There will be no interruption or downtime of service. The only change will be a different supply providers name appearing on your bill in 45 - 60 days. You will still pay the same utility company you always have, we call this a zero habit change service.

Today's economy is difficult at best so you owe it to yourself, at your residence and/or small business, to see if you can save money. You have nothing to lose and only savings to gain.

Mike Menihan

As a seasoned business expert, with 37 years in the Telecommunications Industry, Mike has managed various organizations at AT&T during the Telecommunications Deregulation era, in the 1980's & 1990's.

Mike has also managed various organizations at Emerald Solutions, Inc. and Global Crossing, LLC.

Mike has been a small business owner from 2001 to present.

He entered the energy market in early 2010, currently holds the position of National Consultant with America Approved Energy Service Direct.

To see if you have a choice in your utility market simply contact:

Michael Menihan

973-998-4062

How A Private Investigator Can Help You Get Money

Alexander Toia, PI

The role of today's Licensed Private Investigator is vastly different from what you see in the movies or on television. This chapter will focus on how the role of the Private Investigator, or "PI" can help you in this economy. The value and benefits that a Licensed Private Investigator can bring to the table are listed below:

Locating Assets

Whether you are looking to locate the assets of a debtor (pre- or post-judgment), potential investor, pre- or post-divorce, or after the death of a loved one, PI's have the resources to uncover assets.

Many people are unaware they have a legal permissible purpose to locate assets prior to obtaining a judgment if a debt is owed to them, or that when a loved one passes away, they have the right, as next of kin or executor of the estate, to locate unknown bank, brokerage, and investment accounts.

On your behalf, a private investigator can find; real property (residences, vacation homes, rental properties), motorized vehicles (automobiles, motorcycles, watercraft, aircraft, recreational equipment), personal businesses, bank accounts, brokerage accounts, investments, and safe deposit boxes.

Background Investigations

Before entering into a financial agreement with a potential new partner, a background investigation can help you save considerable money in the long run. Knowing their business, civil, and criminal history will reveal whether or not this is the person with which you want to share your financial resources and business partnership.

Hiring a nanny? Knowing the person you are considering leaving with your children with for hours at a time cannot be measured in terms of their safety, security, and welfare. Carefully choosing the right individual and verifying credentials is paramount. And you would be surprised to find out how it can be relatively economical with a reputable investigator.

Check the records of potential contractors prior to forwarding them an advance fee, ensuring that you are dealing with a reputable company, and knowing the principal's correct full name. Also, signing a contract that makes them personally liable, and verifying that their company is the safest way to approach your project.

Background Investigations are very unique assignments and require private investigators that know how to apply your circumstances to do the job right. While basic investigative and research techniques are employed, the investigator must be highly skilled in assessing and analyzing information, as well as, developing and following leads. Understanding your problem and properly preparing the investigation are the most essential elements of every assignment.

Backgrounds include, but are not limited to, the following:

Address History
Business Ventures
Civil Litigation History
Criminal History
Driving History
Employment
Expert Witness Backgrounds
Investment Opportunities
Pre-Employment
Public Records
Reconstruction of Activities
Resume Verifications

Finding Loved-Ones

Do you need to locate a child you gave up for adoption, or are you looking for your biological parent(s)? Do you have a medical necessity to find either? Whether you need an organ or bone marrow transplant, or your family medical history, a private investigator can help find lost family. As a Licensed Private Investigator in the state of New Jersey, I had an assignment to locate a client's daughter who was given up for adoption 45 five years ago at the tender age of 15. Through my efforts, I was able to locate the daughter with only a first name and date of birth, and arrange a meeting for her and the client. Other services include reuniting old high school and college friends and military buddies.

Establishing Residency to Prove Co-Habitations

When questions arise about how much money you are paying a former spouse in alimony or child support, clients like to know if another person resides there without your permission. If your ex-spouse is residing or cohabitating with an adult, you may have justification to decrease the amount you are paying in support. Private investigators can look for evidence to prove the permanent residential arrangement, which could significantly benefit you financially.

In New Jersey, for example, if a former spouse is cohabitating with another person, same or opposite sex, you may file a motion and request your payments be decreased or terminated throughout the term of that relationship. As a Licensed Private Investigator in the state of New Jersey, I was able to save a client more than $450,000 by showing that his ex-wife had been living with a female partner for many years, even though she claimed to reside alone.

Estates and Wills

There are several important reasons an investigator is hired in probate of a will or when a person dies intestate (without one). Heirs must be identified and located in order to probate or legally process the document. If the person dies without one, a reasonable effort must be made to find next of kin in order for the County Surrogate to release the deceased's personal assets.

When people die in questionable circumstances, or as a result of an accident, family members, insurance companies, and estate lawyers might want to know what events precipitated, caused, or contributed to the death. If a person was unduly influenced, or of unsound mind, to execute a new will, such as a holograph (handwritten and legal), which could supersede an existing legal document, there would also be grounds for investigation to determine relevancy. While investigators cannot legally evaluate legal competency issues, we can still interview people that knew the deceased and can testify to his mental condition and behaviors prior to death.

Electronic Bug Sweeps

When you suspect that your adversaries, opponents, and rivals may know too much about your professional and personal lives, it's time to sweep your location. A private investigator can help locate illegal listening devices and "bugs" in your home, workplace, vehicle, or telephones. Investigators can also inspect your car for GPS (Global Positioning System) tracking devices, which are generally uploaded to satellites while you drive and monitored by computer in real or post time. Additionally, trained and experienced PI's can inspect you hard drives, not only on your computer, but also in your cell phone. As a Licensed Private Investigator in the state of New Jersey, one of my cases involved the checking of a computer and cell phone pertaining to a suicide case that produced evidence to question the validity of the death.

Pet Investigations and Recovery

Similar to lost loved ones, investigators use the same skills and techniques to find lost pets. As a Licensed Private Investigator in the state of New Jersey, a client's 12 year old dog was stolen by people that had a conflict with the elderly couple. Since they had no children, their dogs were treated as their offspring. The lived on a large piece of property where their five dogs could roam, and their prized possession was seized because of a disagreement. The staff of our company pitched in and contacted people they knew in the media. The Star Ledger, Daily Record, and Channel 7 Eyewitness News in New York City, picked up the story and ran with it for a week. The clients offered a $2,500 reward for information leading to the safe return of their beloved pooch. Two people came forward with information that resulted in the reunion of the dog with the family. The clients were so elated they gave each of these people $2,500 and threw a party for 100 people at their home. This is a true story, and I have the news video to prove it!

Alexander Toia, PI

Alexander Toia & Company has the resources to satisfy your investigative needs across the United States and beyond its borders. If you have any questions about how a private investigator may help you, please visit www.atoiacompany.com or call Alex Toia or Barbara Rudd at 973-538-3338.

Professional Careers of Private Investigators - Alexander Toia & Barbara Rudd

Alex Toia, CCLA, LPI began his private investigation career in 1973 while a graduate student at Rutgers University, School of Criminal Justice. He worked part-time as an apprentice investigator for Hamilton Detective Agency, Livingston, NJ that specialized in matrimonial surveillances and missing persons. In 1975, Alex was appointed to New Jersey's newly created Pre-Trial Intervention Program, supervised by the Morris County Probation Department and Prosecutors Office. Background and pre-sentence investigations, defendant and witness interviews, and extensive evaluations were routinely prepared for assistant prosecutors and criminal court judges.

After three years with Morris County, before Special Investigation Units were introduced to the insurance industry, Chubb Insurance Group offered Alex a unique field investigator position to expand its Claims and Litigation Departments. For the next five years, Alex investigated all personal and commercial coverage lines, including motor vehicle claims, construction accidents, property and liability claims, personal injuries, natural and suspicious deaths, and premises liability cases. He also completed a three-year Legal Insurance course at the American Educational Institute to earn the Special Designation of Casualty Claim Law Associate (CCLA), which gives him substantial knowledge of insurance-related litigation few investigators possess.

In 1982, Alex founded Search Investigations, Inc. and specialized in insurance claims, civil litigation, and criminal defense investigations. Clients included insurance carriers, law firms, lawyers, private and public corporations, and self-insured groups throughout the New Jersey/New York Metropolitan area.

After 16 years of successful operation, Alex looked for greater, more complex challenges and merged his company with another investigative agency to form Murphy Toia Murphy, Inc. After almost five years as the company's Internal Operations Director, Alex decided to re-establish his own company where he would have full control of all internal and external operations, and could truly make a positive difference in people's lives. Hence, Alexander Toia & Company, LLC was formed.

Alex is a member of four well noted associations:

ACI	Association of Christian Investigators
NALI	National Association of Legal Investigators
NCISS	National Council of Investigators & Security Services
NJLPIA	New Jersey Licensed Private Investigator Association (Chair of Membership Committee and Editor of its Newsletter, "The Surveillant")

Alex Toia has also published articles in the NALI periodical, PI Magazine, and NJLPIA.

Alex Toia
973-538-3338
alex@atoiacompany.com.

Free At Home Assistance For Veterans & Their Spouses

by Bonnie Laiderman

There is a very little known program called "aid and attendance" for veterans and their spouses (or surviving spouses) In order for veteran's spouse to receive the program benefits the veteran needs to also be ill. This only for veterans who have served at least 90 days active duty during war time for: World War II, Korean War and Vietnam War. For other wars there are other programs. A secondary qualifier is that you need to have a serious medical condition. The third qualifier is income and assets. The primary formula is that the medical expenses need to exceed income. Home and car are excluded as assets. You do not need to sell off assets to qualify or mortgage your home. The goal is to keep people out of nursing home. By providing: light housekeeping, laundry, meal preparation, bathing, food shopping, drive to the doctor visits. The maximum number of hours on average for single veterans – 70 hours a month, for couple – 84 hours a month and for the surviving spouse it is – 45 hours per month.

Also, services can include pairing with the appropriate home nursing services by contracting with companies such as Comfort Keepers.

Bonnie Laiderman

Bonnie Laiderman has a broad range of professional experience that spans several decades in the medical care industry and general business. She began her career as payables supervisor at Jewish Hospital in St. Louis, and quickly was promoted to billing manger, responsible for over $100 million in receivables and nearly two dozen employees. She then became credit manager and was responsible for all collections for the hospital. She opened an automotive import/export business, which she owned for 18 years. The company garnered recognition that included the Governor's Exporter of the Year Award and 1998 Exporter of the Year. In 2003, Bonnie founded Veterans Home Care.

The idea for Veterans Home Care came to Bonnie after the passing of her own mother, Edith Sperling, the widow of a Korean War veteran. Bonnie discovered late in Edith's battle with cancer, that a little-known Veterans Administration pension existed to help pay for home care for veterans or their surviving spouses. Unfortunately, by the time Bonnie was able to apply for the pension on Edith's behalf, it was too late. Bonnie realized that many veterans or spouses were not aware of, or were unable to apply for the pension without assistance. Within a few months of Edith's death, Bonnie opened Veterans Home Care to help deserving veterans obtain the pension.

Veterans Home Care helps veterans and their surviving spouses who qualify, apply for a pension, known as "Aid & Attendance," which pays for assistance with activities of daily living in their homes. Veterans Home Care provides home care, assigns attendant care workers and follows up to assure that the veteran remains in compliance with VA guidelines to continue receiving the pension. There are no out-of-pocket costs to the client; VHC furnishes a zero-interest loan for the cost of home care until the application is approved and VA reimbursements begin. Veterans Home Care has helped more than 3,500 veterans or their surviving spouses to access VA benefits for the care they need. The company currently maintains 11 offices, serving clients in 15 states. The company has been recognized by Inc.5000 as one of America's fastest growing companies for 2009 and 2010, and is Better Business Bureau accredited. Bonnie also serves on the board of ITNAmerica (Independent Transportation Network) ITNAmerica, an organization which provides low-cost transportation to elderly who can no longer drive.

bonnie@veteranshomecare.com
Veterans Home Care
11861 Westline Industrial Drive, Suite 750
St. Louis, MO 63146
314.514.2444 office
800.640.7988 fax
www.veteranshomecare.com

Government Benefits For Low Income Individuals

by Dr. Darsi Beauchamp, Ph.D.

TYPES OF MEDICAID

"Medicaid provides health insurance to parents/caretakers and dependant children, pregnant women, and people who are aged, blind or disabled. These programs pay for hospital services, doctor visits, prescriptions, nursing home care and other healthcare needs, depending on what program a person is eligible for."

You must be:

1. A family with children who are dependent on you.
2. A person who is 65 years or older or a blind person or a permanently disabled person.
3. Or a woman who is pregnant.

Medicaid can be extremely useful for children with disabilities. The coverage is impressive in that it covers the doctors, therapists, eyeglasses, dental, and medicines the children need, as well as home care and respite. Legal resident immigrants must have been in the United States at least five (5) years before being considered, however, if their children were born here, then they are eligible again depending on income guidelines. Immigration exceptions exist, please refer to the list on the website or simply call or visit your county social services office. Remember that income and assets are taken into consideration and that children are eligible only up to the point they reach their 19th birthday.

NJ Family Care

This type of Medicaid is for families who are low income and are in need of health care. This health care can have a co-pay or it can be free. Parents must provide proof of income along with other pertinent documents. Assets are not taken into consideration just income. The coverage depends on the monthly income and size of the family.

The coverage is based on an HMO and applicants will be able to choose the covering company, such as Amerigroup, Horizon Blue Cross and Blue Shield, HealthFirst, and/or United Health Care. The coverage may end for both the parents and the children when the children reach the age of 19 years of age.

All applications are available via the online state website, through the mail (in many languages) or by visiting your county social services office. http://www.njfamilycare.org/index.html

NJ Kid Care

Is for children only who are under 19 years of age whose family qualifies for free or low cost healthcare services. The services are the same as those for NJ Family Care, except that this type of care has four plans and is only for the children, not for the parents. Plan A, B, C, and D. Plan A is for low income families whose children qualify at no cost. Plan B is for families with higher income, and Plan C is for families whose income requires a cost share. Plan D is for children whose families have an annual income of up to $58,450 (family of 4) and must pay monthly premiums.

Medically Needy Medicaid

For families whose income and assets are too high and exceeds the criteria for NJ Family Care or NJ Kid Care. This type of Medicaid allows the family to offset the income by being able to spend down with medical and other care expenses and in cases when a child has a disability and there are typical siblings, then the income can be offset to the typical child in order to help the disabled child qualify. Furthermore, this type of Medicaid may also have a monthly premium and/

or co-pays. In some cases teenagers who live on their own may be able to apply for themselves and may be eligible up to age 21.

Residential Medicaid

This type of Medicaid allows people with disabilities and who are in need of long-term care such as a nursing home and/or any other institution receive services and supports. There is a five (5) year look back provision for eligibility.

Home and Community Waivers for Medicaid

Waivers Services created by Congress as a part of the Social Security Act since 1965 to waive some original Medicaid requirements in order to allow individuals with disabilities to receive home and community services and supports to continue to live at home and participate in the community. The waiver Medicaid program may qualify an individual who may not otherwise qualify under the Standard State Medicaid program. There must be a doctor's order and the person need not be permanently disabled. The supports may include a personal assistant in the home to help with functional situations such as dressing and bathing. In addition to vehicle modifications, transportation, case management, day programs, respite, transitional services, and personal emergency response systems.

AIDS/HIV

This waiver is for people of any age who have Aids or children up to age 13 who are HIV positive. The services are numerous and also may include placement in a foster home and even reimbursement to DYFS.

Community Resources for People with Disabilities

This waiver allows the person with disabilities to be able to continue to live in the home and become integrated into the community without having to be bound to an institution.

Traumatic Brain Injury (TBI)

This waiver allows people who have experienced traumatic brain injuries from ages 21 to 64 to take advantage of the waiver in addition to full Medicaid benefits.

Community Care

This waiver is for people with disabilities who are registered with the Division of Developmental Disabilities (DDD) and whose disability was manifested before the age of 22 years of age.

Long Term Care Global Options

For people 65 years or older or disabled individuals of ages 21 to 64 who are deemed to have a disability by the Social Security Administration, Division of Medical Assistance and Health Services, Disability Review Section. People with chronic mental illnesses and developmental disabilities are not eligible under this category. The services include: "assisted living/adult family care, respite care, home based supportive care, environmental accessibility adaptations, personal emergency response systems, home delivered meal service, caregiver/participant training, social adult day care, special medical equipment and supplies, chore services, care management, transition services and transitional care management, transportation, and attendant care."

Nursing Facility Transitional Global Options

Same as the long-term care options, but for individuals in a nursing facility that are to transition back into the community.

Work Options (NJ Work Ability Program)

People with disabilities of ages 16 to 64 can work and earn up to $50,000 a year and not lose their Medicaid benefits.

However, they may have to pay a small premium to continue with eligibility.

SOCIAL SECURITY DISABILITY PROGRAMS

Supplemental Security Income (SSI)

For children and adults (and those of age 65 or older) who have not worked, individuals who are blind, or disabled with limited income and resources. This type of program is non-taxable and has a work incentive available. Your income cannot go over $2,000 a month to continue to qualify. This plan comes with Medicaid for life.

Social Security Disability Insurance (SSDI)

For adults who have worked. This type of program is taxable and has a work incentive available. You can receive even if you receive worker's compensation. Medical condition or combination of impairment preventing substantial work for at least 12 months or expect to result in death. Determination is based upon age, education and work experience.

To qualify you must have worked 40 quarters of coverage which equates to 10 years of work. For example, $1,200 of earnings gives you one credit or 4 quarters a year.

If a parent becomes disabled, child becomes entitled to funds, but entitlement ends at age 19.

If child is disabled, you must file at 16½, and before 19 years of age. Widows and widowers can collect as early as age 50 for their disabled deceased spouses.

Social Security Retirement is at 75% if you retire at age 62 (1943-1954), 100% at age 66 (1937-1943), and 132% at age 70 (1960+). Under full retirement you can earn up to $14,160, over that you pay $1 for every $2 you earn; At full retirement age you can earn $37,680, over that you pay $1 for every $3 you earn; at the month of full retirement, you have no limit on what you can earn annually. Widows and widowers can collect their spouses social security at age 60 and collect their own at age 66.

For more information visit www.socialsecurity.gov

MEDICARE

For adults 65 years old or older or younger with a particular disability (after 24 months of SSDI) or end stage renal disease, Amyotrophiclateral Sclerosis, Dialysis, and Exposure Environmental Health Hazards (must apply three (3) months before the 65th birthday). This program has a Plan A, B, C, and D. Plan A is hospitalization benefits, Plan B is for outpatient and physician services (this has a premium of about $110.50 a month), Plan C is for Advantage Medicare Plan-Combination of Plan A and Plan B, but with approved private insurance companies. Plan D is the prescription drug coverage.

Medicare has co-pays, deductibles, and co-insurance expenses, because of the gap in pay. There is Medigap, a supplemental insurance as well as others offered by private companies.

SPECIAL NEEDS TRUST

Consult an attorney about a special needs trust. However, a special needs trust is needed in order to allow a person with disabilities to have funds set aside for them. If the funds are in any other type of account, then the person with disabilities may indeed lose their Medicaid and or Supplemental Security Income. Also inquire about how a will may affect a person receiving these government programs.

Get Special Education Help for Students with Disabilities at No Cost

by Dr. Darsi Beauchamp, Ph. D.

SPECIAL EDUCATION[1]

Special Education is a necessary subject in the lives of our children in the United States (U.S.). The Supreme Court decision, Brown vs. Board of Education of Topeka, changed the face of politics and the educational arena. However, before 1965, there was a scarcity of any procedural safeguards for students with disabilities. In 1965, the Elementary and Secondary Education Act, PL 89-10 and the State Schools Act, PL 89-313 were enacted and provided funds to schools to help with the education of children with disabilities.[2] In 1968, the Handicapped Children's Early Education Assistance Act, PL 90-538 was enacted to provide funds for children with disabilities in early childhood settings.[3] In 1973, the Section 504 of the Rehabilitation Act was enacted and helped people with disabilities defend their civil rights with institutions that received federal monies in addition to providing access to people with disabilities equitably.[4] This

---

1 20 U.S.C. § 1401(29) "The term 'special education' means specifically designed instruction, at no cost to parents, to meet the unique needs of a child with a disability, including:
a) instruction conducted in the classroom, in the home, in hospitals, and institutions, and in other settings; and
b) instruction in physical education."

2 Most programs trained children outside of the public schools. Students were deemed as "retarded" or of having "emotional disturbance." This law began providing grants to states so that they could service the children with disabilities.

3 Landmark cases: *Pennsylvania Association for Retarded Citizens v. Commonwealth (1971) and Mills v. Board of Education of the District of Columbia (1972).*

4 The Section 504 Rehabilitation Act is all inclusive of anyone having any disability at any age.

Act, which is still in effect today, provides accommodations to students and people with disabilities. This Act also helped students with disabilities become integrated in schools and have access to activities and buildings. In 1975, the Education for All Handicapped Children Act (EHA), also known as PL94-142 was enacted in response to the treatment of students with disabilities in institutions and schools. This Act made special education mandatory in the United States.[5] In 1986, EHA was reauthorized as PL99-457 to now be inclusive of children under age two (2) with disabilities and to create the Individual Family Service Plan (IFSP) for early intervention. In 1990, the American with Disabilities Act (ADA) provided protections from discrimination stemming from the Civil Rights Act of 1964 under five titles.[6] Under the Clinton administration in 1997, EHA became the Individuals with Disabilities Education Act (IDEA), PL 105-17 and was revised under the Bush administration in 2004 and No Child Left Behind (NCLB) was also added. In 2008, the Children's Defense Fund has indicated that 15% of our 3 year olds are enrolled in state Pre-K, Head Start or special education program and that 38.8% of our 4 year olds are also enrolled in those programs[7].

IDEA

The EHA had been enacted to provide students with dis-

---

[5] "Before this time only one out of five children with disabilities were educated, more than 1 million children were refused access and more than 3.5 received ineffective instruction." Children began to receive a free and appropriate education (FAPE).
Stainback, Susan Bray; Stainback, William C. (1996). *Support Networks for Inclusive Schooling: Interdependent Integrated Education.* Paul H Brookes Pub Co. ISBN 1-55766-041-7. OCLC 300624925.

[6] Title 1 - from discrimination in the employment arena, Title 2 -from public services and transportation, Title 3 - public accommodations (including schools), Title 4 - from telecommunications, Title 5- other provisions-Department of Justice, 2009.

[7] Children's Defense Fund, Washington, D.C. 2008.

abilities access into the public schools. IDEA on the other hand provided that researched based interventions and methods be used as well as a full participation in the public school system which also included independent living skills, eventually leading to a self-sufficient economic life for children with disabilities. IDEA assured students received services from ages 3 to 21 in the school system. IDEA also added new categories to the disabilities range, such as autism, traumatic brain injury, and Attention Deficit Hyperactivity Disorder (ADHD). IDEA presented that a functional behavioral assessment (FBA) and a behavioral intervention plan (BIP) be provided to students whose behavior stood in the way of their learning and the learning of their peers[8]. Furthermore, IDEA also added transition plans to help students with disabilities transition from secondary schools to adult life or even into higher education or post secondary education.

NO CHILD LEFT BEHIND (NCLB)

No Child Left Behind (NCLB) is a revision of the Elementary and Secondary Education Act of 2001 PL 107-110. This Act requires that schools, teachers, and administrators have an accountability of how the students perform in the schools, including children of special and bilingual education. Inclusive is to have highly qualified teachers teaching the students[9] and adequate yearly progress of students. The Act, although under revision in the current administration, required that school districts reach a 100% proficiency in the areas of math and reading by the year 2012. Thus, each state has developed goals and objectives or benchmarks for each grade level and each subject matter and tests in these areas,

---

[8] *20 U.S.C. §§ 1412(A)(14), 1453(c)(3)(D)(v); 20 U.S.C. § 1414(d)(3)(B)(i); 34 C.F.R. § 300.346(a)(2)(I); 20 U.S.C. § 1415(k)(1)(B)(i); 34 C.F.R. § 300.520(b)(1)(i), (ii); and N.J.A.C. 6A: 14-3.7(c)(3)*

[9] Highly Qualified Teachers means that they must be certified/licensed accordingly to teach the area of specialty and grade level-U.S. Department of Education, 2010.

which are now published for parents to peruse. This Act also added the Assistive Technology Act (ATA) of 2004, PL 108-364. The ATA provides funds to schools to purchase assistive technology that will help students with disabilities in their educational endeavors, but also in their transition phase within their individualized education plan (IEP). The funds are divided into different Titles: Title I- Improving the Academic Achievement of the Disadvantaged, Title II - Preparing, Training, and Recruiting Highly Quality Teachers and Principals, Title III - Language Instruction for Limited English Proficient and Immigrant Students, Title IV - 21st Century Schools, Title V - Promoting Informed Parental Choice.

FAPE and LRE

Under IDEA, children have many laws that protect them.[10] Some of the laws and regulations, in other words rights, include LRE[11] and FAPE. LRE is the Least Restrictive Environment and FAPE is Free Appropriate Public Education. FAPE is deemed as having a child receive the proper educational program that is intended for their individual needs and in which the child is prepared in school educationally, for employment and independent living skills[12]. For one thing

---

[10] Federal laws are under the 20 U.S.C. Chapter 1414 and 1415 and 34 C.F.R. Chapter 300. New Jersey State Laws are under N.J.A.C. 6A Chapter 14, under the 1973 Rehabilitation Act-ADA 504 federal laws-Department of Justice, 2009.

[11] *Oberti v. Board of Ed. of the Borough of Clementon School Dist.*, 995 F.2d 1204 (1993)
M.C. v. Central Regional School District, 81 F.3d 389 (1996)
T.R. v. Kingwood Township Board of Education, 205 F.3d 572 (2000)
Cedar Rapids Community School District v. Garret, 526 US 66, 119 S.Ct. 992 (1999)
Irving Independent School District v. Tatro, 468 US 883, 104 S.Ct. 3371 (1984)
Honig v. Doe, 484 US 305, 108 S.Ct. 592 (1988)
Ridgewood Board of Education v. N.E., 172 F.3d 328 (3d. Cir., 1999)

[12] *Knox v. O'Brien*, 7 N.J. Super. 608 (1950)
Board of Education of Hendrick Central School District v. Rowley, 458 US 176 (1982)

FAPE is an appropriate program, not the best program. In other words the U.S. Supreme Court deemed that children of special education were entitled to an appropriate program not the best possible program[13]. As parents we feel that we want the best for our children, but sometimes the best in education may be viewed as over the top and school districts must assure that the child's educational program provides a learning environment in which the children will make meaningful progress educationally. This also means that the child, no matter the disability, has the ability to learn and requires the opportunity to do so. Under FAPE, there are other procedural safeguards such as related services. Related services are services that a child may need to help with their disability as well as in support of their disability. Some of these programs are: Speech/ Language Therapy, Physical Therapy (PT), Occupational Therapy (OT), Psychological services, parent training, health services, transportation, transitional services.[14]

BILINGUAL EDUCATION[15]

Title VI of the Civil Rights Act of 1964 provided rights to students in need of bilingual education (Also called English Language Learners-("ELL") or Limited English Proficient-("LEP") and English as a Second Language (ESL).[16] This Act

---

[13] *Board of Education of Hendrick Central School District v. Rowley*, 458 US 176 (1982)
Individuals with Disabilities Education Act, 20 U.S.C. 1400 et seq.
Rehabilitation Act of 1973, 29 U.S.C. 794
Family Educational Rights and Privacy Act, 34 C.F.R 99
Federal Implementing IDEA Regulations, 34 C.F.R. 300; *and New Jersey Special Education Administrative Code*, N.J.A.C. 6A:14-1 et seq.

[14] *20 U.S.C. § 1414(c)(1)(A); 34 C.F.R. § 300.533(a)(1) and N.J.A.C. 6A: 14-2.5* (c)(4)

[15] *Elementary and Secondary Education Act of 1965*, as amended, Title III, Secs. 3111–3141; 20 U.S.C. 6821–6871; 34 CFR 76.

[16] Bilingual Education Program – A full-time program of instruction in all those courses or subjects which a child is required by law or rule to receive, given in the native language of the children of limited English proficiency enrolled in the program and also in English. The program offers the aural comprehension,

provides rights to access based on color and race. Nonetheless it was not until the Supreme Court decision of Lau v. Nichols, that made headway in helping Chinese students in the San Francisco, California area overcome their language barriers and access to education.[17] In New Jersey, when there are 20 students of a particular language with needs, bilingual education must be provided.[18] Parents have a right to sign to have their children serviced and also have a right to sign their children *out of the program.* Nonetheless, the two prong situation arises when the student is in need of bilingual education and of special education services and the schools may not have the appropriate personnel to service the children. It is important to note that the law requires equal access and protection, therefore, the students must receive testing in their native language (students may have difficulty with these tests, since they have not been instructed in that language and are deficient and even illiterate in that language-therefore results may not be optimal), instruction in their native language when the materials should also be offered to parents in their native language and there should be an interpreter in the IEP meeting.

---

speaking, reading and writing of the native language of the children of limited English proficiency enrolled in the programs, and the aural comprehension, speaking, reading and writing of English; the history and culture of the country, territory or geographic area which is the native land of the parents of children of limited English proficiency enrolled in the program; and the history and culture of the United States. All pupils in bilingual education programs receive English as a second language instruction. English as a Second Language (ESL) Program – A daily developmental second language program which teaches aural comprehension, speaking, reading and writing in English using second language teaching techniques and incorporates the cultural aspects of the pupils' experiences into their ESL instruction. English Language Services Program – These are services designed to improve the English language skills of pupils of limited English proficiency. These are in addition to the regular school program and have as their goal the development of aural comprehension, speaking, reading and writing skills in English. State of New Jersey Department of Education, 2010.

[17] *Lau v. Nichols*, 414 U.S. 56 (1974); Section 1703(f) of the EEOA of 1974; See *Castaneda vs. Pickard*, 648 F. 2d 989 (5th Cir. 1981).

[18] *N.J.S.A.* 18A 35-18 et seq.

EARLY INTERVENTION PROGRAM (EIP)

Early Intervention is a service for children with disabilities or delays from birth, who are eligible from 0 to 3 years of age. A family coordinator is sent to the home to plan with the family and come up with an Individual Family Service Plan ("IFSP"). A social worker is also sent to the home to offer service referrals to the parents. Language Interpreters are available with the state upon request. The services may include: physical therapy, occupational therapy, speech and language, nursing, special education services, Applied Behavioral Analysis ("ABA") therapy services to name a few. The IFSP provides for you information on who will be providing the services, when and how often the services will be provided, and the goals and objectives for the child regarding the services. The service providers are experts in the areas of services and come to the home and provide services according to the IFSP. Every month the service coordinators have a family training meeting to provide the family with an update on the goals and objectives from the plan (explaining growth) and which new goals and objectives will be worked on for the following month. The family service coordinator meets with the family every six (6) months to review and renew the IFSP to determine new goals and objectives and the amount of hours should be increased or decreased for the therapies. When your child is close to 3 years of age, the family coordinator will have a transition meeting with the school's Child Study Team (CST) (please be aware that you need to register your child in the school district where you are domiciled before the coordination with the Child Study Team begins). The family coordinator also sends the child's records with a summary report to the CST for their review.[19] The family coordinator may also participate in the initial

[19] All records from the Early Intervention Family Coordinator must be sent to the school 120 days before the child reaches age 3.

IEP meeting to help develop the initial IEP for your child. The services under this program are free, but some fees may apply according to family resources. If the family is of low resources, they can also apply for Supplemental Security Income ("SSI") from the Social Security Administration ("SSA") for the child, which is also paired with Medicaid[20] to pay for additional services and medical care. Lastly, when the child turns three (3) years of age, the family coordinator sends the early intervention case to the state's Home Care Program which commences during the transition from early intervention to the school district. The Home Care Program assigns a case manager who will coordinate continuing therapy services (various hospitals offer the therapy services) via telephone calls and not necessarily visits the home.[21]

PRESCHOOL

As we mentioned before all children with and without disabilities are to receive a Free and Appropriate Public Education ("FAPE"). Children who have disabilities can begin school at age three (3).[22] Pre-School children with disabilities must be treated the same as any school age child. They are eligible to be in the Least Restrictive Environment ("LRE"), therefore, have a right to be educated with their peers, unless, the IEP Team (inclusive of the parents) decide that the child will benefit from a Pre-School Handicapped program. Nonetheless the code is clear that children with disabilities should be placed with their peers and be in an all inclusive program to the maximum extent possible. In addition, the children should be evaluated and the IFSP should become

---

[20] Medicaid provides free transportation to all medical services and therapies.

[21] At age 5 years of age, mental health services are available to students via the Perform Care Services.

[22] Please be aware that you need to register your child in the school district where you are domiciled before the coordination with the Child Study Team begins.

a record as well as any evaluation from a health care provider or specialist which has indicated that the child has a disability and recommendations by those specialists. The school district can conduct their own evaluations, but cannot decline other evaluations. Furthermore, once the parents sign to consent for evaluations the school has 90 days to conclude the evaluations and to provide the student with an initial IEP. The programming must be ready to be implemented by age three (3). This means that in order for the school district to conform to having the child begin school by age three (3), they must begin the referral and evaluations 120 days before the child becomes three (3) years of age.[23] Nonetheless, the initial IEP cannot be implemented if the parents do not sign it. However, the parents can sign as participants and for the eligibility as well as to commence services, but still can invoke the 15 days to review the IEP. If within the 15 days, the parents do not agree with the district they can succour to (depend on) the procedural safeguards such as mediation and due process. Once the child turns three (3), the school district cannot deny him/her entrance to school, especially knowing that the child has a disability.

HOW TO QUALIFY FOR SPECIAL EDUCATION

REFERRAL

Once you, a doctor, a teacher, an administrator, anyone refers (in writing to school principal and/or director of special education) a student to the Child Study Team ("CST") for evaluations, the CST has 20 days to coordinate a meeting with the parents and the entire IEP Team to discuss the referral and to make a determination to evaluate. Remember you can suspect not always know there is a problem with a student not making proper progress in school.

---

[23] Educational Law Center:The Right To Special Education in New Jersey: A Guide for Advocates, 2008.

IEP TEAM

The IEP Team consists of: the parents, a school psychologist, a learning disabilities teacher consultant (LDTC), a social worker, a special education teacher, a general education teacher, a speech therapist (if warranted), a physical therapist (if warranted), an occupational therapist (if warranted). One of the providers, whether the school psychologist, the LDTC or the social worker will also become the case manager for the IEP team. There could be a representative from the school district which can very well be a principal, vice-principal, director of special services, or the board attorney (if warranted), these members must also be knowledgeable on supervision and the curriculum. However, any member must be familiar with the child and the child's educational strengths, weaknesses, and performance. If a child is 14 years and over (the child with disabilities can be in school until age 21) they too can also be a member of the IEP Team. In addition, in order to coordinate services with pertinent agencies, a representative of those agencies can also be present, especially if they are coordinating transition services for the student. Furthermore, a parent has a right to bring an expert, friend, relative, advocate or attorney to the IEP meeting.

MEETINGS

All meetings should be notified by mail and another adequate form to the parent with copies of a proposed IEP and/or evaluations to the parent 10 days before the IEP meeting. The notification should indicate the date, time, location, reason and who will be attending the IEP meeting. All IEP meetings can be recorded by the parent. There is no need to ask permission, however, out of courtesy to the school district and so they too can have the same opportunity to record, they should be informed in advance.

EVALUATIONS

Initial evaluations are done when the child is in school (except for the initial evaluation - see the Pre-School section) within the 90 calendar days time frame after the parents have signed a consent to evaluate. While the evaluations are going on within those 90 days, the school can provide interventions as developed by the Intervention and Referral Services Team ("I&RS"). However, the I&RS Team cannot stand in the way of the referral to the Child Study Team. The Child Study Team should also include the school nurse in the initial evaluation to provide the student with a physical assessment and medical referrals if necessary to rule out any medical conditions that may be standing in the way of the child's learning. Including evaluations done by a neurologist or a neurodevelopmental pediatrician. If the child's behavior stands in the way of his/her learning and the learning of others, then a Functional Behavioral Assessment ("FBA") and Behavioral Intervention Plan ("BIP") shall be conducted again with the consent of the parents, because it is an evaluation. Teachers can use different forms of evaluations in the classroom to document if the interventions they have attempted to use with a child have been working or if despite the interventions the students still have problems in progressing. The tests for assessment in the classroom are: DIBELS (Dynamic Indicators of Basic Literacy Skills), DRA (Developmental Reading Assessment), WIAT (Wechsler Individual Achievement Test), CBM (Curriculum Based Measurements), RTI (Response to Intervention-CBM is a part of this as well). All evaluations that are conducted at the school district are done at the expense of the public school system.

---

[24] All students who cannot participate in the statewide assessment are Alternate Proficiency Assessment ("APA") to demonstrate progress via the performance of the Core Curriculum Content Standards ("CCCS") within a portfolio of work

RE-EVALUATIONS

All re-evaluations are done within a three (3) year time frame to demonstrate the growth of the child and to reformulate the IEP. Re-evaluations can occur sooner if warranted. The school district has 45 days to conduct the re-evaluations. The results should be provided to parents in an IEP meeting where new goals and objectives as well as short-term benchmarks are developed.[24]

INDEPENDENT EDUCATIONAL EVALUATIONS (“IEE”)

During the discussion of the evaluations or re-evaluations, if the parents are not in agreement with the results; the parents can then invoke in writing their right to IEE's. The school district has 20 days to respond to the parents whether they will accept the IEE's or whether they will then file a due process hearing defending their evaluations. If the school district does not file for a due process hearing, they then must provide the parents with a list of providers that are just as qualified as the school evaluators, in other words with the same qualifications and certifications. The parents can choose from the list or can choose an independent evaluator from outside the list. The IEE's are at public expense and the parents do not pay for them. Even if the school district files for a due process, the parents can still have the independent educational evaluations done, but must pay for them out of pocket. Nonetheless, the IEE's recommendations and summaries must be taken into consideration by the school district. No school district can interfere with an IEE as per federal code.[25] The school district or the school board attorney cannot ask the independent evaluators to refrain from

---

products from the student. APA students must have short term individualized goals that are reflective of the student's current level of performance devised from the evaluations.

[25] 34 C.F.R. § 300.502(b)(1) and (2); N.J.A.C. 6A:14-2.5(c)(2)(i) and (ii).

[26] State of New Jersey Department of Education IEE criteria sent to all districts.

providing recommendations or which test to administer.[26] This would be construed as an interference. It is not advisable for parents to have the independent evaluations done in the school setting in order to avoid interference and in order to give the student the opportunity to perform outside of the school district. Unless the evaluator must observe the student in the school to gather data for their report or are evaluating the child's programming and placement. The IEE's should be done at the office of the evaluator or in the home of the child or at an approved site per code. If for any reason the evaluation being requested by the parent has not been done by the school district, then the school district has 45 days to evaluate the child and if the parents are still in disagreement, they can still have the IEE done at public expense. Remember that no independent evaluator can be employed by the district in which the child is domiciled, but an evaluator from another district can evaluate the child. You are only entitled to one independent evaluation in each area that you are in disagreement with every time the school district performs an evaluation or re-evaluation that you disagree with. A student should be evaluated every three (3) years, but does not have to be if both the parents and school district agree to waive the evaluations.

CLASSIFICATION

Once the IEP Team determines that a child is eligible for special education services, they must determine which of the 13 categories the child falls under to receive proper educational interventions. For complete determinations, see N.J.A.C. 6A:14-3.5, this is an excerpt of the listing under this code.

CLASSIFICATION	ACRONYM	DETERMINATION
Specific Learning Disability	SLD	Perceptually impaired-in language, imperfect ability to listen, think, speak, read, write, spell, math calculations.

CLASSIFICATION	ACRONYM	DETERMINATION
Speech and Language Impairment	SI	Speech disorder in articulation, phonology, fluency, voice, or any combination.
Other Health Impaired	OHI	Chronically ill-disability characterized by limited strength, vitality, or alertness in educational environment due to chronic or acute health problems.
Emotional Disturbance	ED	Multiple characteristics in intellectual, sensory, health, interpersonal relationships, and behaviors or feelings that are inappropriate, pervasive mood of unhappiness or depression, tendency to develop physical symptoms or fears
Auditorily (Hearing) Impaired	AI/HI	Inability to hear within normal limits
Autistic	Autistic	Pervasive Developmental Disability impacting verbal and non-verbal communication, and social interaction which adversely affects a student's performance
Cognitive Impaired (three levels included see below)	CI	"Mentally retarded"- significant below average general cognitive functioning
1. Mild Cognitive Impairment	CI-Mild CI	Educable-level of cognitive development and adaptive behavior - mildly below age expectations

CLASSIFICATION	ACRONYM	DETERMINATION
2. Moderate Cognitive Impairment	CI - Moderate CI	Trainable - level of cognitive development and adaptive behavior - moderately below age expectations
3. Severe Cognitive Impairment	CI - Severe CI	Eligible for day training cognitive development and adaptive behavior - severely below age expectations
Communication Impairment	Communication Impairment	Communication handicapped - language disorder in areas of morphology, syntax, sematics, and/or pragmatics/discourse, not due to auditory impairment.
Multiply Disabled	MD	Multiply handicapped, multiple disabilities, two or more disabling conditions
Deaf/Blindness	D/B	Concomitant hearing and visual impairments = severe communication
Orthopedically Impaired	OI	Severe orthopedic impairments
Pre-School child with a disability	Pre-School Handicapped	Between ages 3 and 5 with developmental delay
Social Maladjustment	SM	Inability to conform to standards of behavior established by school
Traumatic Brain Injury	TBI	Neurologically Impaired - injury caused to the brain by external force or insult to the brain.
Visually Impaired	VI	Visually Handicapped - impairment-even with correction

INDIVIDUALIZED EDUCATIONAL PLAN ("IEP")

The IEP must be developed within 30 calendar days from the determination that a child is eligible for special education and the related services determined by the evaluations. Parts of an IEP are as follows:[27]

1. Strengths and areas to be addressed academically, developmentally, and functionally
2. Any concerns the parents may have about their child's education
3. Any results from assessments and evaluations
4. Behavioral interventions for students whose behavior stands in the way of their learning and the learning of others
5. ESL or LEP classes for children with limited English proficiency.
6. Blind or visual impairment-Braille instruction in coordination with the Commission for the Blind.
7. Communication needs
8. Academic levels
9. Assistive Technology devices needs and services
10. Involvement of DDD
11. Involvement of DVRS from age 14 or younger or other agencies
12. Statement of present levels of academic achievement
13. LRE-involvement in general education and how disability affects involvement and progress
14. Measurable annual academic and functional goals and short term goals if APA

---

[27] School districts use IEP software templates. However, the basic ingredients of an IEP arc listed under the IEP template provided by the State of New Jersey-Department of Education-Special Education Service link: http://www.state.nj.us/education/specialed/form/

15. Supplementary aids and services

16. Related Services

17. Individual modifications

18. Frequency, location, duration of related services and modifications

19. From age 14 to 21, graduation requirements and how student is expected to meet

20. Types of assessments and any modifications

21. Transitions elementary to middle, middle to high school, high school to work world, including social, academic, and vocational statements

22. At age 16 or younger, measurable post secondary goals, which include training, education, and employment

23. Independent living or community participation also included

24. Progress of goals and objectives

25. How parents will be informed of progress

26. Information on out of district placements and how student will participate with nondisabled peers

27. How District will include participation of agencies at IEP meetings

28. Meetings annually to review and review IEP

29. Review of annual goals

30. Review of re-evaluations if any

31. Classroom/teacher assessments review, state assessments, observations, etc

32. Any new needs as presented by IEP Team, inclusive of parents and teacher

33. Review of out of district placements if can come back, transition to least restrictive environment

34. Signatures of those who participated in IEP meeting

35. Remember that the IEP must first be completed before placement is decided

36. The school district may bring forth to the meeting an outline of what will be offered, however the IEP must be developed during the IEP Team meeting.

37. The proposed IEP and any evaluations must be sent to the parents 10 days before the meeting along with a notice of meeting.

EXTENDED SCHOOL YEAR ("ESY")

This part of the instructional aspect of a child's IEP demonstrates that during the summer months, the child may regress and how long would student take to recover or that a part of the child's learning needs to be continued or that their behavioral or physical conditions warrant the related services. The usual time frame is for the entire month of July. Some programs can go up to the second week of August in private schools.

PLACEMENT

The goals, objectives, the statements, the entire IEP must be developed before placement can be determined. Remember that the IEP is a legal working document that can be amended at any time, even if when the placement is determined new benchmarks can be added.

SECTION 504 ACCOMMODATION PLAN

Students who do not qualify under IDEA and have disabilities qualify for the American with Disabilities Act ("ADA") Section 504 Rehabilitation Act, however, all children who qualify for IDEA also qualify under Section 504.[28] The Section 504 also covers adults in the work environment. A disabled person under ADA "has a physical or mental im-

[28] A student can have both, an IEP and a Section 504 Plan.

pairment which substantially limits one or more major life activities; has a record of such impairment; or is regarded as having such an impairment." The children have a disability, but not a learning disability or impairment. Usually an ADA Section 504 Accommodation Plan is used for students who have physical impairments (permanent or temporary) or asthma, epilepsy, allergies, ADHD, diabetes, central auditory processing problems, physical therapy and occupational therapy needs, any related services or accommodations or modifications or special education services that are not eligible under an IDEA with an IEP. The students are still required to have FAPE and LRE just as in IDEA. A Section 504 committee meets to evaluate the needs of a child and to receive the medical documentation from parents to prepare a plan. The recommendations of the health care provider are taken into consideration and provided in the plan.

GUARDIANSHIP

Means providing the protection of a person who is incapacitated or incapable of making financial, educational, and medical decisions on their own. The children are usually of 18 years old when the custody of children ends for the child's parents. The incapacitated child does not have the capability of managing their own affairs.

Children's guardianship can also be obtained by a person other than a parent in special circumstances with minor typical and a typical children. The parents do not lose their parental rights, however the guardian is the person to make the decisions in the upbringing of the child, up until the Court deems the guardianship is no longer needed and is no longer in the best interest of the child or children.

However, the Courts appoint a court appointed attorney

[29] The Court appointed attorney is an additional expense to that of the advocate or attorney preparing the guardianship.

who will interview the parties mentioned in the verified complaint.[29] The Courts in New Jersey also require a 90 day accounting report and an annual report to be submitted by the guardians.

PROCEDURAL SAFEGUARDS

MANIFESTATION DETERMINATION

A special education student is not excused from school rules or board regulations for behavioral issues. However, a special education student is entitled to a manifestation determination meeting to determine whether or not the act committed stemmed from their disability. If the act committed stemmed from their disability, then the student is entitled to a manifestation determination and then a board hearing with the board of education to present their evidence on their behalf. If the act committed does not stem from the disability, then the student may receive the same suspension as a student in regular education. Nonetheless, if a parent does not agree with the manifestation determination, they can attend the board hearing and go further with an expedited due process hearing within 20 days after hearing is filed. The administrative law judge ("ALJ") makes the determination within fifteen (15) days from the time the due process is received.[30] Any time a special education child is suspended for ten (10) school days, there may be a change of placement. This means that a school can place the child in an alternative setting for 45 days. If the school filing to end the placement is the out of district school, that school cannot unilaterally end the placement.

MEDIATION

This avenue is used to have a state employee who is trained in mediation attend a mediation meeting with the two parties

---

[30] Their is No Stay Put when you file due process of a manifestation determination or any changes in placement due to disciplinary proceedings.

in dispute. The state employee is employed by the Department of Education, Office of Special Education Programs ("OSEP") and is an impartial party who is at the meeting to help assist the parties with the dispute in reaching an agreement. The OSEP mediators are knowledgeable of the federal and state codes under IDEA, N.J.A.C.6A-14 et seq., and ADA. The mediation unlike the court mediations are at no cost to the parents. The parents may bring with them experts, an attorney or an advocate. The Stay Put provision is also valid during the mediation procedure. If mediation does not become the viable solution and a school district maintains that they want to remove the student from their placement or not enforce the IEP, then the parents can file for emergent relief.[31]

EMERGENT RELIEF

This provision is a serious procedural safeguard and one must provide evidence that the removal or non-compliance can cause the child "irreparable" harm before a full hearing is heard. The stay put provision comes into play at this point until the matter is heard either in the emergent relief hearing, or transferred to the due process avenue and this has concluded.[32] The parents must provide evidence that the irreparable harm will occur if the relief is not granted, legal right of claim is settled, that the claim can stand on its own merits, or that the child will suffer harm more than the school district if they cannot acquire the relief.

DUE PROCESS

If you file for emergent relief for one issue and your petition has several other issues that are not a part of the emergent

---

[31] Any time a parent mails any packet of mediation, emergent relief, due process to a school district or OSEP, it should be sent via the quickest viable mailing and certified to keep copies for your records of who and when the documents were received.

[32] Stay Put is automatically provided with the emergent relief or due process provision. As long as the case is accepted based on its merits with OSEP and transferred to OAL.

relief, they then become a part of the due process. During the due process, a resolution meeting is scheduled within 15 days of receipt of the packet by all parties. During the resolution meeting, all parties must be in agreement to record the meeting. If the parents have an attorney, then the board attorney may be present. If the parents are represented by a non-attorney advocate, then the board attorney cannot be present. The case manager, the director of special services, the supervisor of special education, even the superintendent may be present. However, this is not an IEP team meeting, so the child study team should not interfere with the process. This is not about offering services or to develop an IEP or to argue about the petition. This meeting is to discuss the issues presented to the state by the parents on how the disputed issues can be solved as written in the petition. Once the issues are agreed upon, a settlement agreement is drafted by hand that day of the meeting. The formal settlement agreement can be drafted by either party. If the day of the resolution meeting, the issues are still outstanding or only part of the issues are still outstanding, the case can be scheduled for a conference with the judge at the office of administrative law in Newark or Trenton, depending on the location of the school district. The judge will give another opportunity to have the pending issues discussed and come to a resolution that day in court. If the issues are not resolved that day, then the judge will schedule the case for a hearing. Usually the parties can have access to the assigned administrative law judge on the telephone for phone conferences to help resolve the issues. Experts, witnesses, and discovery of documents are a part of the due process procedures, as well as subpoenas of teachers and other school staff.

If the case is settled upon an agreement, the board of education must vote on a resolution that will be sent to the court so that the court can approve the settlement agreement with an order from the judge. If the settlement agreement is not adhered to, the parents can return to court to have it enforced.

Reimbursement of attorney fees can be formally sought if the parent has prevailed during the due process hearing.

COMPLAINTS

Parents are entitled to file a complaint investigation with the Department of Education. The complaint is based on violations of the federal or state code within one year of its occurrence. The Department of Education will investigate within 60 days. The facts are presented to the state and the determination is made within the 60 days. If for any reason the parents also file a due process petition, the due process procedure must first occur before the state begins the complaint. At this point, the state will provide an "exceptional circumstances" extension of time until the due process procedures have concluded. If the issues are resolved and rectified during the due process procedures, then the decision of the court or the settlement agreement is binding. If there is only a complaint investigation, then the state may visit the district and interview parties and compile records to make the determination on how the district can compensate the child with corrective procedures. The Department of Education will also provide the school district technical assistance on how to correct the outstanding issues. If the parents want to appeal the complaint investigation results, they must do so via a due process, for there is no appeal process of complaint investigations. A two year period is the allotted time to file due process commencing with the date of the filed complaint.

COORDINATING WITH AGENCIES IN NJ

It is important for parents to note that all children with disabilities must be registered by them with the Division of Developmental Disabilities ("DDD") for them to apprise the child for services. The Division of Vocational Rehabilitation Services ("DVRS") is a consultative body for students 14 years of age and older to help in the transition phase of students with disabilities from school to work programs. The DVRS will conduct vocational assessments for high students with disabilities to better understand and propose a work plan according to the child's strengths, needs, and aspirations. Both the DDD and DVRS should be invited by the school to IEP meetings. In addition, the DVRS in coordination with other agencies depending on the disability of the student will devise a transition plan that will help teach the student in the areas of assistive technology, vocational assessments, community based instruction (provided by the school district), transition instruction (provided by the school district), independent living skills, and social skills.

LIST OF AGENCIES AS PROVIDED BY THE NJ EARLY INTERVENTION SYSTEM (Reproduced with permission of NJEIS, 2010).

Statewide Agencies:

Advocacy:

Disability Rights New Jersey, (800) 922-7233; www.drnj.org
Statewide Parent Advocacy Network (SPAN, (800)654-SPAN; www.spannj.org
Education Law Center; www.edlawcenter.org
NJ Coalition for Inclusive Education, (732) 613-0400; www.njcie.net;
Wrights Law, www.wrightslaw.com

Assistive Technology

NJ Protection & Advocacy, (800) Dial-Tec; www.njpanda.org
NJ Coalition for the Advancement of Assistive & Rehab Technology, http://www.njcart.org/
Rehabilitation Technology Services and Technology Lending Center (CPNJ), (888) 322-1918
Disability Resources for Assistive Technology, http://www.disabilityresources.org/AT.html
Assistive Technology Center (Advancing Opportunities) http://www.assistivetechnologycenter.org/tlc/tlc.php
Family Resource Connection, Inc., http://frainc.org/techconnection/

Child Care:

NJ Inclusive Childcare Project, (800) 654-7726 x108; www.spannj.org/njiccp
County Childcare Resource and Referral Agencies, (800) 3-329-2273; www.njaccrra.org

Disabilities:

The Arc of New Jersey, (732) 246-2525; www.arcnj.org
Council on Developmental Disabilities, (800) 216-1199; www.njddc.org
Division on Developmental Disabilities, (800) 832-9173; www.state.nj.us/humanservices.ddd
National Information Center for Children & Youth with Disabilities, (800)695-0285; www.nichcy.org

Early Intervention:

New Jersey Early Intervention System, (888) 653-4463; www.njeis.org

Education:

NJ Dept. of Education, (609)292-4469; www.state.nj.us/education
NJ Dept of Early Childhood Education, 609-777-2074; www.nj.gov/education/ece
Head Start Programs, www.state.nj.us/humanservices/oece/head_start.htm
NJ Dept. of Special Education, (609)292-4469; www.nj.gov/education/specialed
The Learning Resource Centers, (609)292-4469; www.nj.gov/education/lrc
Individuals with Disabilities Education Act (IDEA) www.ideapractices.org
Family Support:
Family Support Center of NJ, (800) FSC-NJ10; www.fscnj.org
NJ Self-Help Clearinghouse, (800) 367-6274; http://www.njgroups.org
Exceptional Parent Resource Guide, (800) E-Parent; www.eparent.com
Options Manual (800) FSC-NJ10; www.fscnj.org

Health Care:

Community Health Law Project (888)838-3180; http://www.chlp.org
Family Voices (Health Issues): (800)654-SPAN x110
www.familyvoices@spannj.org
NJ Family Care (Health Coverage) (800)701-0710 www.njfamilycare.org
Parent to Parent Support:
National Father's Network; www.fathersnetwork.org
NJ Statewide Parent to Parent: (908)537-467; email: parent2parent@spannj.org

Social Services:

Women, Infant and Children (WIC) (800) 328-3838
www.state.nj.us/health/fhs/wic/index.shtml
Division of Youth and Family Services (DYFS) 877-652-2873;

www.state.nj.us/humanservices/dyfs Special
Child Health Services (888) 653-4463
Supplemental Security Disability Insurance (800) 772-1213; www.ssa.gov

Transition Resources:

Boggs Center, (732) 235-9300; http://rwjms.umdnj.edu/boggscenter
National Early Childhood Technical Assistance Center (NECTAC); www.nectac.org

The following is an informal listing of resources that have information about services and supports that many families may find useful. The NJEIS does not endorse any content, program, product or methodology found on any of their listed websites. All resources were accurate at the time of printing.

DISABILITY RELATED/SPECIFIC RESOURCES:

Autism:

Autism NJ, (800) 4-Autism; www.autismnj.org (formerly COSAC)
Autism Speaks, (888) 777-6227; www.autismspeaks.org
Autism Society of America, (800)328-8476; www.autism-society.org
Visual Impairment:
Commission for the Blind and Visually Impaired (973)648-3333 (Central Office); www.state.nj.us/
humanservices/cbvi/home
National Federation of the Blind, (410)659-9314; www.nfb.org
American Foundation for the Blind, (800)232-5463; www.afb.org

Cerebral Palsy:

Cerebral Palsy of NJ (Advancing Opportunities), (888) 322-1918; www.cpofnj.org
United Cerebral Palsy of Northern, Central and Southern NJ, 908-879-2243; www.ucp.org/ucp_local.cfm/100

Hearing Impairment:

Division of Deaf and Hard of Hearing, (800)792-8339; www.state.nj.us/humanservices/ddhh

Down Syndrome:

National Down Syndrome Society (NDSS), (800)221-4602; www.ndss.org
National Down Syndrome Congress (NDSC), (800)232-NDSC; www.ndsccenter.org
The Arc of NJ, (732)246-2525; www.arcnj.org

The Judy Center for Down Syndrome (healthcare); (201)996-JUDY
Down Syndrome Association of Central NJ, (866) 369-6796; www.dsacnj.org
Down Syndrome Web Page; www.downsyndrome.com

Fragile X Syndrome:

The National Fragile X Foundation, (800)688-8765; www.FragileX.org
The Fragile X Association of NJ, www.fragilex.org/htm/new_jersey.htm

Rare Disorders:

Rare Disorders, http://www.rare-disorders.com/
Disability Resources; http://www.disabilityresources.org/RARE.html

Spina Bifida:

Spina Bifida Assoc. of the Tri- State region, (908)782-7475; www.sbatsr.org

Sibling Resources:

The Sibling Support Project, (206)297-6368; www.siblingsupport.org
Parents and Agencies Supporting Siblings (PASS); (908)537-4673
Frequently Asked Questions Siblings Need to Know About their Brother or Sister with Special Needs: For a copy, contact Mid-Jersey Cares REIC (732)937-5437
Transition Resources:
"Special Needs Successful Inclusion: A Guide to Planning Community Activities for Children with Special Needs": To order, go to www.cnjmchc.org
NECTAC: Transition www.nectac.org/topics/transition/transition.asp
NECTAC: Inclusion www.nectac.org/inclusion

"We do the same things over and over, expecting different results." Albert Einstein

"You must do the thing you think you cannot do."

Eleanor Roosevelt

"........But laws and institutions must go hand in hand with the progress of the human mind. As that becomes more developed, more enlightened, as new discoveries are made, new truths discovered and manners and opinions change. With the change of circumstances, institutions must advance also to keep pace with the times. We might as well require a man

to wear still the coat, which fitted him when a boy as civilized society to remain under the regimen of their barbarous ancestors."

–Thomas Jefferson

How to Get an Amazing Education For Low to No Cost

Dr. Darsi Beauchamp

College expenses are on the rise in the 21st Century. Nonetheless, college can be free for many if they qualify. It all begins with good marks in high school. By having a good standing and a good grade point average (GPA), a student can be eligible for many programs. One such program is NJ STARS. A student must be a resident of New Jersey and must be the top 15 percent of their graduating class. The Edward J. Bloustein Distinguished scholars scholarship is for high school seniors which will attend an approved college or university.

Scholarship or grant monies are available to use in studies in different areas. Such as health care, law enforcement, teaching, accounting, sciences, etc. Each college and university have their own scholarships and/or grants. The Free Application for Federal Student Aid (FAFSA) must be filled out *every year* by each student, otherwise you may not be considered for financial aid. In addition, state universities (in New Jersey for example) such as Rutgers State University, Montclair State University, The College of New Jersey, Kean University, New Jersey City University, Ramapo College, Richard Stockton College, Rowan University, Thomas Edison State College, and William Paterson University have more scholarship and grant opportunities than private colleges. Needless to say that county colleges also have a lot of opportunities. In addition, county colleges offer a variety of approved two-year programs at lower costs than four year universities. County colleges can also be a saver, in other words, the two year colleges can be cost effective in the first two years of a Bachelor's degree. Make sure the courses are approved by the four-year college you want to attend. County colleges offer a variety of courses both during the school year and the summers that can count towards any major at a lower cost. In addition, when you attend a two-year college and then apply at a four-year college you will be considered a transfer student. This means that you are not competing with the general population, but only with yourself and this allows you better chances in getting into a four-year university with only two more years to pay for. During this time a person who takes courses at a two-year college, has the ability to do well and maintain a higher grade point average. The higher grade point average will help you get into honor societies and receive scholarship or grant monies as well to go into the four-year university.

Furthermore, many foundations exist where they provide monies based on need or merit. These foundations have criteria and deadlines that must be strictly adhered to or your chances to qualify will decline. There are foundations that are based on the area of study or just based on your heritage and even on your name. The choices are endless and millions of dollars go unclaimed every year. The monies are available for undergraduate, graduate, doctoral programs, and post-doctoral (graduate) programs.

There are many websites that can help you begin your quest, you may begin with this one and continue to search state and federal and specific school scholarships and grants. http://www.studentscholarshipsearch.com/Scholarships/Local_Scholarships/United_States_Scholarships/New_Jersey_Scholarships/more2.php

If you are unemployed, check with your reemployment agency for a review of your skills set. The agency may be able to retrain you in another area. Grant monies are also available to attend approved schools and are paid for by the Department of Labor and Workforce Development.

Dr. Darsi D. Beauchamp

Dr. Darsi D. Beauchamp has had extensive training in the area of education and administration. She holds a bachelor's in Psychology and one in Spanish/French from Rutgers University with certifications in both New Jersey and California to teach grades Pre-K-12th as well as, a Master's in Counseling (Family Therapy focus) from California Polytechnic and another Master's in Educational Administration/Business Administration from Montclair University. In addition, she has a doctorate (Ph.D.) in Educational Administration from Capella University in Minnesota, which she has used in managing schools, companies, and government agencies in the private and public sectors. Furthermore, she has years of experience in the areas of marketing, human resources/employment law, counseling, teaching, and translations. She is fluent; bilingual and bi-literate in Spanish and conversant in French. Her Behavior Analysis Certification is from Saint Joseph's University in Philadelphia.

Some of her employment opportunities and doctoral program have allowed her to be involved in the development of curriculum in differentiated instruction to help all students (Pre-K-College and private companies) in the area of learning interdisciplinary comprehensive studies. Her philosophy is that "all students have the ability to learn, given the right opportunity, skills, strategies, and environment." She has trained many teachers in this methodology and in supervision and is a Staff Development Provider with the New Jersey Department of Education. She has also provided workshops and forums in the areas of curriculum development, conflict resolution, and special education.

Her dissertation is published in the Journal of Biology, Neurology and Education for her contributions in how the brain learns and interacts with the environment, thus promoting lessons that tap into the children's curiosity, by holding their attention, while using all their senses in learning; taking into consideration their learning needs and pace. Recently, she has changed careers and delved into the area of law by becoming a Paralegal (Fairleigh Dickinson University, Madison, NJ) and is working with different agencies in the areas of disabilities and employment law. Her goal is to go on to law school to continue her contributions in school and employment law. She is also a court appointed mediator trained by the New Jersey Association of Professional Mediators (NJAPM) and a non-attorney advocate.

She is a member of the American Association of University Women, New Jersey Association of Women Business Owners, NJ State Chamber of Commerce, Latin-Vision, Hispanic Chamber of Commerce, Alpha Epsilon Lambda, National Association of Elementary School Principals, National Association of Judiciary Interpreters and Translators, New Jersey Association of Paralegals, Universidad de Salamanca, Association for Supervision and Curriculum Development, NJ Special Education Providers, New Jersey Association of Professional Mediators, and the American Red Cross.

Advanced Learning was established in 1992 and DDB Productions in 1988.

Advanced Learning and DDB Productions
P.O. Box 302
Morris Plains, New Jersey
advocacy@advancedlearningddb.net
973-400-9794

I Owe the IRS... *HELP!*

by Jack Bleiberg, CPA

At some point, many taxpayers find themselves in the uncomfortable situation where they find that they owe taxes that they cannot pay when due. Panic sets in. Some people resort to denial and think that they can hide, and just do not file at all. Others get "creative" on their returns and file what may even be a fraudulent return. And, then there are still others that file a correct return and pay what they can at the time. A few write a tearful note in the hope that a kind person will come to their rescue.

Moreover, if you owe money to the IRS, there is an excellent chance that you also owe money on the state level. All states handle this differently. I practice in New Jersey, but the basic advice is the same for all taxing authorities. So let's discuss the reactions that I noted above:

- Yes, it is an awful realization. Bear in mind that, unless you have committed tax fraud, filed a misleading document, or tried to avoid tax altogether (ala Al Capone), the enforcement is financial and you *will not go to jail!* Further, within reason, you will not be forced to live on the street and you will be allowed to buy the basics of life. If you live an extravagant life style and owe a large tax bill, you may be forced to adjust that life style (ask Willie Nelson).

- No, you can no longer hide. The IRS and the states compare information automatically. It is a certainty that if income is reported via a W-2, 1099, or similar document, all taxing authorities will know about it and compare it to your returns. That being said, you may find that the taxing authorities may not been able to reconcile similar income originating from multiple sources. In that case, although you may have properly reported income, they will send you a bill. Just reply, in writing, with a full explanation and they will correct their records.

• Do not get creative by fabricating events (charitable contributions, medical expenses are being scrutinized) that you cannot substantiate. Always report all of your income. Underreporting income is the most serious source of tax fraud.

• If you cannot pay your tax, *do file the return in a timely manner*. Given that you cannot successfully hide forever, be aware that there are two levels of penalties. One is late or non-filing, the other is underpayment of tax. By filing the return, you at least avoid the late filing penalty. By paying a small amount, you can prove that the return was received on a timely basis, as the payment will indicate the date processed. Also, many jurisdictions allow payment by credit card. If your cash shortage is temporary, this may be less expensive than tax interest and penalties. You may even be able to get frequent flyer or similar benefits from the credit card company. You need to compare your credit card rates with the then current government rates. If it's even close, pay by credit card.

All of this being said, understand that no one is trying to harm you. The agencies are highly automated. Notes attached to the return will not be read or get a response. The underpayment will generate a notice that you did underpay, add interest and a late payment penalty, and include a date that the resulting balance is due. That due date is important to the extent that more interest and penalty will accrue after that date. If you can now pay the tax, pay it. If not, I recommend that you visit the taxpayer assistance center of the IRS or similar state facility. The IRS lists the locations and hours of these centers at http://www.irs.gov/local contacts/ index.html (be aware that many of these centers close for an unpublicized lunch hour, so call ahead and confirm your timing). This is where the human being enters the picture. Bring the notice with you and explain your circumstances to the agent. They normally establish a *multi-year payment plan* with *monthly payments*. This does not stop the interest or penalties from accumulating, but it does stop their collection actions. Check with them, but most of the time, this is not reported to credit rating bureaus. It is all very civil and friendly. The key is that you came forward voluntarily and were not trying to avoid payment of the tax. However, you must be absolutely sure that you pay all monthly installments on time, or the arrangement is cancelled and they will aggressively restart collection proceedings, including the possible seizure of your bank accounts. On the other hand, if your financial position improves, pay it off early to avoid the interest and penalties.

If you do chose to visit the taxing authority, *you do not need to bring your accountant* or attorney along with you as long as you speak English and can understand the payment plan proposed. However, if you are nervous or need an interpreter, then you may want that assistance. Typically, you are charged for their time, so think that through.

Finally, consider what events happened that resulted in you owing such a large balance. You want to correct that situation so that it is not an annual event. Generally, a new payment plan will not be offered unless you have no existing plans and are current on all other taxes. If substantially all of your income is from wages or salary, you may not have the proper amounts withheld from your paycheck. It is far easier to have a small part of the tax bill withheld each payday than to come up with a large amount once a year. You withholding is based on the form W-4 that you filed with your employer when you were hired. It specifies your marital status and the number of dependents that you will claim. If that changes, you need to submit a new W-4. Ask your employer to furnish you with one.

If you have substantial income that is not subject to withholding (business income, interest, dividends, capital gains, pensions, etc,), you may need to pay quarterly estimated tax installments. These forms (1040-ES) are available on the internet, however I recommend that you see a tax preparer to help you compute the estimate and complete the forms.

In both the case of withholding of taxes from pay and the filing of estimated taxes, be aware that these are estimates. The actual tax return will produce the precise tax amount. There will always be at least a small overpayment or underpayment. Depending on your individual situation, you may want to apply all or a part of any overpayment to the next years tax (as an additional estimated tax payment). It is always easier to pay with money that you did not know that you had, or saw in your bank account.

Frequently Asked Tax Questions

by Jack Bleiberg, CPA

There are some questions that seem to always be asked. I am often surprised that many otherwise knowledgeable people are not aware of the answers, so I took this opportunity to present them. Underlying any tax information is the fact that you are responsible to keep all of your records and receipts for five years, unless fraud is suspected (then, there is no statute of limitations and you will need to prove your assertions). Please also note that each state has nuances of difference form the Federal discussion. For this publication, I am discussing only the Federal considerations, unless stated otherwise. In no way should the contents of this article be considered "tax advice," as that can only be rendered to specific fact sets.

What are Withholding and Estimated Taxes?

Do you sometimes wonder why, at the time of filing your 1040, there may be a large amount due or a refund? When you start a new job and are asked to complete a W-4, do you understand how many exemptions to claim? Withholding and / or estimated tax payments are mechanisms that determine how much tax you pre-pay for the respective year. You are required, by law, to prepay you taxes, or you will be subject to interest and penalty charges. Withholding applies to the classic worker on a company's payroll. Estimates apply to any other significant taxable income and are due in four installments throughout the year, using form 1040-ES. The exemption question on the W-4 allows you to adjust the amount withheld to reflect the tax effects your spouse and all of your dependents. It is impractical to expand this discussion to include when to claim additional exemptions for itemized deductions, or less for other income. I suggest that you consult a tax professional if you suspect that additional exemptions are appropriate.

Should I consider a ROTH retirement plan (IRA or 401-K)

A traditional retirement plan allows you to accumulate money that you have not yet been taxed on.

You pay taxes as the money is withdrawn. In a Roth plan, you accumulate "after tax" money. When you withdraw it, those amounts are tax free. If you believe that your effective tax rate in the current year is less than the tax rate that you will have on retirement, a Roth is for you. For example, if you have earned substantially lower income during the current year that you normally do, consider a Roth. If you are a student, or are just entering the workforce with low earnings, consider a Roth. Bear in mind that current tax rates (2010) are the lowest in decades and are expected to be increased in the coming years.

Are there Retirement Plans for the Sole Proprietor or the Self-employed (and IRA vs. 401-K)?

If you are in your own small business, retirement plan options exist! Even is you are the only person in the company and you are not receiving a paycheck, you may be able to open a "Simple" plan. I always favor the 401-K option. If all goes well economically, the difference is immaterial. However, in hard times, you can borrow up to 50% of your 401-K balance (make sure that the plan is set-up to allow it) and pay it back over several years with interest going to your own plan balance. That gives you a huge avenue of relief, should you really need it. You cannot borrow from an IRA.

What Business Deductions are Available for the Sole Proprietor or Self-employed?

All business related expenses are deductible. Some are subject to limitations. Entertainment and meals are only deducted at 50%. Significant asset purchases (except land) up to $250,000 per year can be deducted, and the remainder can be claimed as depreciation expense over the useful life of the asset class. Vehicles purchased and leased are subject to special rules. The IRS has two helpful publications that can be downloaded from www.irs.gov:

- Publication 334 – Tax Guide for Small Business
- Publication 587 – Business Use of Your Home

These are extremely informative and useful. Remember to keep your receipts and, if entertainment, note on the receipt the purpose of the event and who (if anyone) attended.

Which Types of Business Entity Should I Chose?

This depends on many factors specific to you. In most cases, you should obtain the advice of a tax professional. In order to provide some insight and prepare you for that discussion, these are your choices:

- Unincorporated businesses are businesses for which no formal entity has been established. You are taxed based on the income and expenses as reported on Schedule C of your annual form 1040. The individual is personally responsible for all debts and obligations of the business.

- Partnerships are unincorporated businesses owned by more than one person. A separate form, 1041, must be filed. That form reports the distribution of taxable items between the partners who also receive that information through the schedules K1 of the 1041. The individuals are all personally responsible for all debts and obligations of the business. A Partnership Agreement is required, and a legal name must be approved and registered with the state.

- Limited Partnerships, like partnerships, are unincorporated businesses owned by more than one person. A separate form, 1041, must be filed. That form reports the distribution of taxable items between the partners who also receive that information through the schedules K1 of the 1041. In this case, a class of partners ("Limited Partners") are responsible for the debts and obligations of the limited partnership only to the extent of their investment. There must be at least one "General Partner" who is personally responsible for all debts and obligations of the business. A Partnership Agreement is required, and a legal name must be approved and registered by the state.

- Limited Liability Companies (and Partnerships) are unincorporated businesses owned by one or more persons. If only one person owns it, the income and expenses are reported on the Schedule C of Form 1040. If more than one person owns it, a separate form, 1041, must be filed. That form reports the distribution of taxable items between the partners who also receive that information through the schedules K1 of the 1041. In these entities, all owners are responsible for the debts and obligations of the limited partnership only to the extent of their investment. These are legal entities that must obtain a legal name must be approved and registered by the state. Written agreements between the owners should be documented.

- Corporations (or "C" Corporations) are the traditional corporation which issues stock. The corporation itself is taxed and files Form 1120. Any distributions to shareholders in the way of dividends are taxed again. The shareholders are responsible for the debts and obligations of the corporation only to the extent of their investment. A Stockholders agreement is required, and a legal name must be approved and registered by the state.

- Subchapter S (or "S" Corporations) are similar to "C" Corporations, except that the *income is not taxed at the corporate level, but flows through to the shareholder*s. These corporations file annually on form 1120S, the K-1 of which reports the distribution of taxable items between the shareholders. Income is only taxed once. The shareholders are responsible for the debts and obligations of the corporation only to the extent of their investment. A Stockholders agreement is required, and a legal name must be approved and registered by the state.

Jack Bleiberg, CPA

Jack is a practicing CPA who has a developed proficiency in guiding companies to reach their full potential through proper planning and execution, and maximizing operational efficiencies and controls. He also works with his clients to protect their wealth with proper tax, business exit and estate planning. Jack has worked with all sizes of entities, from small through large public companies.

Jack has been a partner at a regional CPA firm, and owned and operated business systems and consulting firms. Jack has over twenty-five years of experience owning and operating small businesses. He has extensive experience across many industries.

Jack is a graduate of Lehigh University, where he obtained a Bachelors degree in Accounting He has been published in the CPA Journal and chaired a committee of the NJ Society of CPAs. Jack is currently Vice President and Executive Board Member at the Daughters of Israel Geriatric Center in West Orange, NJ. He is a member of the American Institute of CPAs, the NJ Society of CPAs, and is active with the North Essex Chamber of Commerce.

Contact Information: Jack@JBleibergCPA.com
Website: www.JBleibergCPA.com

Veronica L. Yankowski

photographer

Veronica L. Yankowski has been a professional photographer for sixteen years. Most of that time has been dedicated to photojournalism by working with several of the top news organizations in the area including: *The Associated Press, The Star Ledger,* and *The New York Times*. Veronica has accumulated over twenty awards for her work from such organizations as the New Jersey Press Photographers Association, the New Jersey Press Association and the Suburban Newspapers of America. Her most heralded works include her pictorial essay on the aftermath of September 11th and her collection of environmental portraiture.

Muse Productions published "Dialogue 3" in 2002. This led to exhibitions of her work across the state at such venues as the Strand Theater in Lakewood, NJ, and the Monmouth Beach Cultural Center, Monmouth Beach, NJ, to name a few.

In 2003, Chiarascuro Photography was born which blends a dramatic journalistic style with a creative, artistic flair. Veronica comes to the location of your choice and offers unobtrusive photography of children, families, maternity and events. If you are looking for more creative corporate head shots and events, Veronica will bring her creativity to your shoot to make your photos different and unique. She is currently an adult Photography teacher at Brookdale Community College, Lincroft, NJ, teaching courses on how to better use your point+shoot & DSLR cameras.

973-449-6167
www.veronicavision.com
vyankowski@yahoo.com

NOTES

NOTES

NOTES

NOTES

NOTES